E. D. Townsend

Harmonies of the Bible and the Church

E. D. Townsend

Harmonies of the Bible and the Church

ISBN/EAN: 9783337171629

Printed in Europe, USA, Canada, Australia, Japan

Cover: Foto ©Lupo / pixelio.de

More available books at **www.hansebooks.com**

HARMONIES

OF

THE BIBLE

AND

THE CHURCH.

BY

GENERAL E. D. TOWNSEND.

A shadow of things to come; but the Body is of Christ. *Colossians* ii. 17.

Saying none other things than those which the prophets and Moses did say should come. *Acts* xxvi. 22.

1891.

The pages of this book were set up, and printed on a hand press, by the Author himself; which accounts for their typographical imperfections.

Dedicated to the Rev. Dr. GEORGE WILLIAMSON SMITH, President of Trinity College, in memory of a long, and highly valued friendship.

CONTENTS.

CHAP.		PAGE
I.	THE TREE OF LIFE	2
	The Tree, and the Water	4
	The Cherubims, and the Flaming Sword	9
	The Way of The Tree of Life	11
II.	THE COVENANT OF THE RAINBOW	13
	The New Priesthood	18
	The Church	23
	The significance of the Colours	26
III.	TYPES OF THE ATONEMENT	30
	Abel's offering	30
	Isaac	31
	Joseph	35
	The Scapegoat	39
	The Blood Offering	41
	The practical application	42
IV.	THE FIRSTBORN—THE FIRSTFRUITS	44
	The Priesthood of the Firstborn	51
	The Firstfruits	53
V.	CIRCUMCISION AND BAPTISM	56
VI.	THE FEASTS—OLD AND NEW	61
	The Passover—Easter	62
	The Feast of Pentecost—Whitsuntide	66
	The Feast of Tabernacles—Christmas	68

CHAP.		PAGE
VII.	THE TRUMPET.	74
VIII.	THE SEVEN CANDLESTICKS	78
IX.	THE EPIPHANY STAR	85
X.	THE TEMPLE OF THE LORD.	92
	The Tabernacle	92
	The Temple at Jerusalem	95
	The Bride the Lamb's Wife.	98
	The Church Militant	104
XI.	HOLY JERUSALEM.	109
XII.	THE KING OF ISRAEL	116
XIII.	THE WORD	120
XIV.	THE ANGEL OF THE LORD	126
XV.	THE ROCK–THE STONE.	132
XVI.	THE RESURRECTION OF THE BODY	137
XVII.	UNITY.	143
XVIII.	THE BOOK OF COMMON PRAYER	155

PREFACE.

The following chapters may at first glance seem to be nothing but collections of texts with which most persons are familiar; and that very familiarity may prevent a careful reading of every word of them, with a view to discover what is revealed by the entire groups on comparing them together. It is also very necessary that an examination shall be made without prejudice; for nothing is so fatal to a just understanding of any subject, as judgment formed beforehand against it.

Bishop Horsley says:— "It is incredible to any one who has not made the experiment, what a proficiency may be made in that knowledge which maketh wise unto salvation, by studying the Scriptures with reference to the parallel passages *without any other commentary, or exposition*, than what the different parts of the Sacred Volume mutually furnish for each other. Let the most illiterate Christian study them in this manner, and let him never cease to pray for the illumination of that Spirit by whom these Books were dictated, and the whole compass of abstruse philosophy and recondite history shall furnish no argument with which the perverse will of man shall be able to shake this learned Christian's faith."

The typical significance of many parts of the Holy Scripture is no new idea. A reasonable recognition of it cannot fail to add force, as well as beauty, to the scheme of our salvation. It is undoubtedly possible to indulge too far in fanciful interpretation; but there can be but little danger of going astray so long as it points only to the "Bright and Morning Star," the end and hope of our salvation.

It is not pretended that these chapters are exhaustive. They are only suggestive. Perhaps they may be interesting to three classes of persons.

First: To Members of the Protestant Episcopal Church, especially to those who have never fully comprehended the true genius of their own Church.

Second: To members of other Christian Churches. These chapters may show a design and significance in the doctrine and ritual of the Church, which they have not supposed to be so strictly in accord with Scriptural teaching. While they may not be thereby convinced of the necessity of these things, they may yet be led to entertain a greater respect and tolerance for a faith which can thus give a reason for its existence.

Third: To the People of Israel, this book may be offered in the spirit of St. Paul: "Brethren, my heart's desire and prayer to God for Israel is, that they might be saved." *Romans* x. 1.

Both Christian and Israelite may stand side by side on the ground of the Old Testament. The Old Testament cannot be ignored without ignoring as well the very existence of that numerous people. Our own Apostles testify of it that, "All Scripture is given by inspiration of God." 2 *Tim.* iii. 16. And, "Holy men of God spake as they were moved by the Holy Ghost." 1 *Peter* i. 21. Every fascinating form of literature, poetic, historic, descriptive, imaginative, is found in this Scripture. None appreciate its delights more fully than they whose origin, life, and religion it records. Even the humblest of them seem to be familiar with it. It is a characteristic of that people of ancient descent, that their intellects partake of that poetical and imaginative character which is so conspicuous in the Oriental writings. If, then, they could dispassionately and intelligently study the New Testament, in close connection with their own Scripture, the Old Testament, might they not possibly rejoice in realizing that the true stories of their Sacred Scriptures are replete with types and allegories, the explanation and fulfilment of which may be found in ours? This fact once acknowledged by Israel will make them in the strongest sense the chosen of God: chosen, first, to witness of the only true God; and again chosen to eternal salvation, when they shall say, with Andrew, Simon Peter's brother, "We have found the Messias, which is, being interpreted, the Christ." Then, the wondrous and awful sounds from Mount Sinai, which accompanied the giving of the Law, glancing from Mount Zion, (*Ps.* xiv. 7.) the Mountain of the Lord, (*Is.* ii. 2, 3.) will reverberate with a clear and distinct echo of hope and joy, from the great and high Mountain, where sits that great City, the Holy Jerusalem, descending out of heaven from God, with twelve gates, and, "names written thereon, which are the names of the Twelve Tribes of the Children of Israel;" And the wall, "with twelve foundations, and in them the names of the Twelve Apostles of the Lamb." *Rev.* xxi. 9-14.

[The idea of The significance of the Colours, (*Chap.* II.) is mainly taken from "Hitherto, A story of Yesterdays," by Mrs. A. D. T. Whitney:]

City of Washington.
February, 1891.

HARMONIES
OF
THE BIBLE
AND
THE CHURCH.

CHAPTER I.

THE TREE OF LIFE.

———:o:———

In the book of Genesis we read:—

In the beginning God created the heaven and the earth. *Gen.* i. 1.

And God said, Let us make man in our image, after our likeness. *Gen.* i. 26.

So God created man in His own image, in the image of God created He him; male and female created He them. And God blessed them, and God said unto them, Be fruitful, and multiply, and replenish the earth, and subdue it. *Gen.* i. 27, 28.

And the Lord God formed man of the dust of the ground, and breathed into his nostrils the breath of life; and man became a living soul. *Gen.* ii. 7.

The Breath of the Lord God-the Holy Spirit-giving man life, made him in the image of God, without sin, or the knowledge of evil.

And the Lord God planted a garden eastward in Eden; and there He put the man whom He had formed. And out of the ground made the Lord God to grow every tree that is pleasant to the sight, and good for food; THE TREE OF LIFE also in the midst of the garden, and the tree of knowledge of good and evil. And a *river* went out of Eden to *water* the garden. *Gen.* ii. 8-10.

And the Lord God commanded the man, saying, Of every tree of the garden thou mayest freely eat: But of the tree of the knowledge of good and evil, thou shalt not eat of it: for in the day that thou eatest thereof thou shalt surely die. *Gen.* ii. 16, 17.

Thus God, having created man in His own image, left him to enjoy all good things at his pleasure, only forbidding him to seek even the knowledge of evil. Moreover, God distinctly told man that death was the penalty of sin, which would come by disobedience of His command.

Now the serpent was more subtil than any beast of the field which the Lord God had made. *Gen.* iii. 1. [That old serpent, which is the Devil, and Satan. *Rev.* xx. 2.]

And he said unto the woman, Yea, hath God said, Ye shall not eat of every tree of the garden? Ye shall not surely die: For God doth know that in the day ye eat thereof, then your eyes shall be opened, and ye shall be as gods, knowing good and evil. *Gen.* iii. 1, 4, 5.

And when the woman saw that the tree was good for food, and that it was pleasant to the eyes, and a tree to be desired to make one wise, she took of the fruit thereof, and did eat, and gave also unto her husband with her; and he did eat. *Gen.* iii. 6.

And the Lord God said, Behold, the man is become as one of us, to know good and evil: and now, lest he put forth his hand, and take also of the Tree of Life, and eat, and live for ever: Therefore the Lord God sent him forth from the garden of Eden, to till the ground from whence he was taken. So He drove out the man; and He placed at the East of the garden of Eden, *Cherubims*, and a *flaming sword* which turned every way, to keep the *way* of the Tree of Life. *Gen.* iii. 22–24.

There are five significant parts of this allegory:—1st, The Tree; 2d, The Water; 3d, The Cherubim; 4th, The Flaming Sword; 5th, The Way of the Tree of Life. The first and the second are generally found closely connected together.

THE TREE AND THE WATER.

David likens a good man to a tree by the water:—

Blessed is the man that walketh not in the counsel of the ungodly, nor standeth in the way of sinners, nor sitteth in the seat of the scornful. But his delight is in the law of the Lord; and in His law doth he meditate day and night. And he shall be like a TREE planted by the rivers of WATER, that bringeth forth his fruit in his season; his leaf also shall not wither; and whatsoever he doeth shall prosper. *Psalm* i. 1-3.

And Solomon says:—

Happy is the man that findeth Wisdom, and the man that getteth understanding... She is a TREE OF LIFE to them that lay hold upon her. *Prov.* iii. 13, 18.

But there is another significance belonging to the Tree. The Law says:—

If a man have committed a sin worthy of death, and he be to be put to death, and thou hang him on a *Tree*: His body shall not remain all night upon the tree, but thou shalt in any wise bury him that day; for he that is hanged is accursed of God. *Deut.* xxi. 22, 23.

In the Levitical law sacrifices are commanded which, under the Old Testament, were types of the one great, all sufficient sacrifice of the New Testament. The essence of the sacrifice is thus stated:—

The life of the flesh is in the *blood*: and I have given it to you upon the altar to make an atonement for your souls: for it is the *blood* that maketh an atonement for the soul. *Levit.* xvii.11.

St. Paul alludes to this when he says:—

Almost all things are by the law purged with blood; and *without shedding of blood is no remission. Heb.* ix. 22.

But: It is not possible that the blood of bulls and of goats should take away sins. *Heb.* x. 4.

Nor can the blood of sinful man :—

They that trust in their wealth, and boast themselves in the multitude of their riches; None of them can by any means redeem his brother, nor give to God a ransom for him; For the redemption of their soul is precious, and it ceaseth for ever: [*or, as in the Psalter version*, For it cost more to redeem their souls; so that he must let that alone for ever.] That he should still live for ever, and not see corruption. *Psalm* xlix. 6–9.

But Isaiah thus prophesies of Messiah :—

He was wounded for our transgressions, He was bruised for our iniquities: the chastisement of our peace was upon Him; and with His stripes we are healed. All we like sheep have gone astray; we have turned every one to his own way; and the Lord hath laid on Him the iniquity of us all... It pleased the Lord to bruise Him; He hath put Him to grief: *when thou shalt make His soul an offering for sin*, He shall see His seed, He shall prolong his days, and the pleasure of the Lord shall prosper in his hand. *Is.* liii. 5–10.

St. Paul explains this when he says :—

Christ hath redeemed us from the curse of the law, being made a curse for us: for it is written, Cursed is every one that hangeth on a tree. *Gal.* iii. 13.

Here may be noted the minute fulfilment of the type in its several parts. As the law required that the body of him who was hanged on a tree should be taken down and buried that same day, so the body of Jesus was taken down the same day He was crucified. *John* xix. 31.

Again, St. Paul says :—God commendeth His love toward us, in that, while we were yet sinners, Christ died for us. Much more then, being now justified by His *blood*, we shall be saved from wrath through Him. *Rom.* v. 8, 9.

And again: Be ye reconciled to God. For He hath made Him to be sin for us, who knew no sin; that we might be made the righteousness of God in Him. *2 Cor.* v. 20, 21.

And St. Peter told the High Priest:—

The God of our fathers raised up Jesus, whom ye slew and hanged on a *tree*. Him hath God exalted with His right hand to be a Prince and a Saviour, for to give repentance to Israel, and forgiveness of sins. *Acts* v. 30.

Again, St. Peter said to Cornelius:—

God anointed Jesus of Nazareth with the Holy Ghost and with power: who went about doing good, and healing all that were oppressed of the devil; for God was with Him. And we are witnesses of all things which He did both in the land of the Jews, and in Jerusalem: whom they slew and hanged on a *tree*: Him God raised up the third day, and shewed Him openly; Not to all the people, but unto witnesses chosen before of God, even to us, who did eat and drink with Him after He rose from the dead. And He commanded us to preach unto the people, and to testify that it is He which was ordained of God to be the Judge of quick and dead. To Him give all the prophets witness, that through His name whosoever believeth in Him shall receive remission of sins. *Acts* x. 38.

Again, St. Paul said to the people of Antioch:—

And when they had fulfilled all that was written of him, they took him down from the *tree*, and laid him in a sepulchre. But God raised him from the dead. *Acts* xiii. 29, 30.

And St. Peter: For even hereunto were ye called: because Christ also suffered for us, leaving us an example, that ye should follow His steps: Who did no sin, neither was guile found in His mouth:......Who His own self bare our sins in His own body on the *tree*, that we, being dead to sins, should live unto righteousness: by whose stripes ye were healed. For ye were as sheep going astray; but are now returned unto the SHEPHERD and Bishop of your souls. 1 *Peter* ii. 21-25.

The power to overcome that old Serpent, the Devil, through faith in the death of Christ on the Cross, was typified when the people spake against God, and against Moses:—

The Lord sent fiery serpents among the people, and they bit the people; and much people of Israel died. Therefore the people came to Moses, and said, We have sinned, for we have spoken against the Lord, and against thee; pray unto the Lord, that He take away the serpents from us. And Moses prayed for the people. And the Lord said unto Moses, Make thee a fiery serpent, and set it upon a pole: and it shall come to pass, that every one that is bitten, when he looketh upon it, shall live. And Moses made a serpent of brass, and put it upon a pole, and it came to pass, that if a serpent had bitten any man, when he beheld the serpent of brass, he lived. *Num.* xxi. 5-9.

In reference to this Jesus said:—

As Moses lifted up the serpent in the wilderness, even so must the Son of man be lifted up: That whosoever believeth in Him should not perish, but have eternal life. *John* iii. 14, 15.

The type of the TREE OF LIFE is thus shown

to signify the Cross of Christ. If the tradition be true, that the pole upon which Moses hung the brazen serpent was in the form of a cross, there could be no more expressive emblem of St. Paul's saying:—

Our old man is crucified with Him, that the body of sin might be destroyed, that henceforth we should not serve sin. *Rom.* vi. 6.

As a tree draws life and health from water, so from the water of Baptism, springs the grace to be nourished by the Supper of the Lord, the memorial of His crucifixion.

The mention of *water* in connection with a *tree* occurs in several places in Holy Scripture, beside those above quoted.

When the Children of Israel came to Marah, they could not drink of the waters of Marah, for they were bitter: therefore the name of it was called Marah.... And Moses cried unto the Lord; and the Lord shewed him a *tree*, which when he had cast into the waters, the waters were made sweet: there He made for them a statute and an ordinance, and there He proved them. *Exodus* xv. 23-25.

So the broken baptismal vows may be reestablished by worthily receiving the Lord's Supper.

The sons of the prophets said unto Elisha,.... Let us go.... unto Jordan, and.... make us a place there, where we may dwell.... So he went with them. And when they came to Jordan, they cut down wood. But as one was felling a beam, the axe head fell into the water: and he cried, and said, Alas, master! for it was borrowed. And the man of God said, Where fell it? And he shewed him the place. And he cut down a *stick*, and cast it in thither; and the iron did swim. Therefore said he, Take it up to thee. And he put out his hand, and took it. 2 *Kings* vi. 1–7.

This singular miracle was hardly wrought with the simple purpose to gratify the man by restoring his lost property. It probably had an allegorical significance. "Alas, master! for it was borrowed." So may a baptised person say, who sees himself in danger of losing, under the turbid waters of toil or temptation, the grace which he has borrowed in baptism, but has not yet made his own by that other sacrament in memory of the atonement on the accursed *tree*. But the Master shews him the TREE OF LIFE, through which he may recover that grace. Nor only so; He rewards the poor laborer's solicitude for the borrowed instrument, by freely confirming him in its possession, through faithful use of that branch of the *Tree*, the Eucharist.

THE CHERUBIMS, AND THE FLAMING SWORD.

The Cherubims represent the "Ministering Spirits, sent forth to minister for them who shall be heirs of salvation." *Heb.* i. 14.

In the directions for making the Ark of the Covenant, God commanded Moses to make two cherubims of beaten gold, one for each end of the mercy seat, above upon the ark.

And the cherubims shall stretch forth their wings on high, covering the mercy seat with their wings. and their faces shall look one to another... And there I will meet with thee, and I will commune with thee from above the mercy seat, from between the two cherubims which are upon the ark of the testimony, of all things which I will give thee in commandment unto the Children of Israel. *Exodus* xxv. 18–22.

In allusion to this, David says:—

Give ear, O *Shepherd* of Israel, Thou that leadest Joseph like a flock; Thou that dwellest between the cherubims, shine forth. *Psalm* lxxx. 1.

Here is St. Peter's "Shepherd and Bishop of your souls"; He who says, "I am the Good Shepherd: the good shepherd giveth his life for the sheep." *John* x. 11.

So David says:—

The Lord reigneth; let the people tremble: He sitteth between the cherubims; let the earth be moved. *Psalm* xcix. 1.

Ezekiel says of his vision of the cherubims:—

The sound of the cherubims' wings was heard even to the outer court, as the voice of the Almighty God when He speaketh. *Ezek.* x. 5.

St. John says of One whom he saw, "like unto the Son of man:"—

Out of His mouth went a sharp twoedged *sword*. *Revelation* i. 13, 16.

And of the "Word of God," he says:—

Out of His mouth goeth a sharp *sword*, that with it He should smite the nations. *Revelation* xix. 15.

St. Paul says:—

The Word of God is quick, and powerful, and sharper than any twoedged sword, piercing even to the dividing asunder of soul and spirit, and of the joints and marrow, and is a discerner of the thoughts and intents of the heart. *Heb.* iv. 12.

Now St. John says:—

In the beginning was the Word, and the Word was

with God, and the Word was God.... All things were made by Him; and without Him was not any thing made that was made.... And the Word was made flesh, and dwelt among us, (and we beheld His glory, the glory as of the only begotten of the Father,) full of grace and truth. *John* i. 1, 3, 14.

This is He who, in the beginning, created the heaven and the earth. *Gen.* i. 1.

So, He that sitteth between the cherubims, upon the mercy seat, is the Son of man; the Lord who reigneth; the Word who was God; the Shepherd of Israel; the Shepherd and Bishop of our souls. This is He of whom Isaiah prophesied:—
He shall grow up before Him as a tender plant, and as a root out of a dry ground: He hath no form nor comeliness; and when we shall see Him, there is no beauty that we should desire Him. He is despised and rejected of men; a man of sorrows, and acquainted with grief: and we hid as it were our faces from Him; He was despised, and we esteemed Him not. Surely He hath borne our griefs, and carried our sorrows: yet we did esteem Him stricken, smitten of God, and afflicted. *Isaiah* liii. 2-4.

THE WAY OF THE TREE OF LIFE.

Jesus saith unto him, I am the *way*, the truth, and the *life*. *John* xiv. 6.

And St. Paul says:—
Having therefore, brethren, boldness to enter into the holiest by the blood of Jesus, by a new and *living way*, which He hath consecrated for us, through the veil, that is to say, His flesh... Let us draw near with a true heart in full assurance of faith. *Heb.* x. 19-22.

Jesus Christ, the Good Shepherd and likewise the Judge, by giving His life for the sheep, opens to them again the *way* to the *Tree of life*; while, with His flaming sharp *sword*, He drives away from it the sinful people. And this is His promise:-

He that hath an ear, let him hear what the Spirit saith unto the churches; To him that overcometh will I give to eat of the TREE OF LIFE, which is in the midst of the paradise of God. *Rev.* ii. 7.

Blessed are they that do His commandments, that they may have right to the TREE OF LIFE, and may enter in through the *gates* into the city. *Rev.* xxii. 14.

And here are the *gates*:-

Then said Jesus unto them again, Verily, verily, I say unto you, I am the *door* of the sheep.... By me if any man enter in, he shall be saved. *John* x. 7, 9.

When a child is baptised, the minister says:-

And humbly we beseech thee to grant, that he being dead unto sin, and living unto righteousness.... may crucify the old man, and utterly abolish the whole body of sin; and that as he is made partaker of the death of thy Son, he may also be partaker of His resurrection.

The Church also, in the Collect for the Sunday next before Easter, thus teaches us to pray for eternal life through the death and resurrection of Jesus Christ:-

ALMIGHTY and everlasting God, who, of thy tender love towards mankind, hast sent thy Son our Saviour Jesus Christ, to take upon Him our flesh, and to suffer death upon the cross, that all mankind should follow the example of His great humility; mercifully grant that we may both follow the example of His patience, and also be made partakers of His resurrection, through the same Jesus Christ our Lord. *Amen*.

CHAPTER II.

THE COVENANT OF THE RAINBOW.

———:0:———

We read of covenants which God made with man at various times, beginning many thousands of years before the birth of Christ. It is curious to mark how the *water* and the *blood* run through them all, like a cord binding together the whole system.

The first covenant was made with Adam, when the Lord God planted a garden, and made every tree pleasant to the sight and good for food, and a river to *water* the garden; and then gave to man the right to eat of every tree, except the tree of the knowledge of good and evil. Here the covenant was one of *peace*. God's bounty to man is set forth as His part; obedience is man's part. And here, only the fertilizing *water* is found, for as yet the cause for the shedding of blood has not arisen. But after man's disobedience, there appears a *blood* offering as atonement, in Noah's sacrifice. For, when he left the Ark:-

Noah builded an altar unto the Lord.... and offered burnt offerings on the altar. And the Lord smelled a sweet savour; and the Lord said in His heart, I will not again curse the ground any more for man's sake... neither will I again smite any more every thing living as I have done. While the earth remaineth, seedtime and harvest, and cold and heat, and summer and winter, and *day and night shall not cease. Gen.* viii. 20–22.

And God spake unto Noah, and to his sons with

him, saying,... I will establish my covenant with you; neither shall all flesh be cut off any more by the waters of a flood; neither shall there any more be a flood to destroy the earth.... I do set my BOW in the cloud, and it shall be for a *token* of... the *everlasting covenant* between God and every living creature of all flesh that is upon the earth. Gen. ix. 8-16.

Again, God said to Abraham:—
I will establish my covenant between me and thee and thy seed after thee.... for an *everlasting covenant*, to be a God unto thee.... This is my covenant, which ye shall keep, between me and you and thy seed after thee; Every man child among you shall be circumcised.... it shall be a *token* of the covenant betwixt me and you. Gen. xvii. 7-11.

Circumcision was the token of the old covenant of atonement by *blood*. The heads of families, or tribes, then served as priests for their own families. As a first step towards an established priesthood:—

The Lord said unto Moses, Gather unto me *seventy* men of the elders of Israel, whom thou knowest to be the elders of the people, and officers over them; and bring them unto the tabernacle of the congregation, that they may stand there with thee. And I will come down and talk with thee there: and I will take of the Spirit which is upon thee, and will put it upon them; and they shall bear the burden of the people with thee, that thou bear it not thyself alone. Num. xi. 16, 17.

Afterwards, when the Lord instituted the system of worship for the Church of Israel, He commanded Moses, saying:—

Take thou Aaron thy brother, and his sons with him from among the children of Israel, that he may minister unto me in the priest's office, even Aaron, Nadab and Abihu, Eleazar and Ithamar, Aaron's sons. *Ex.* xxviii. 1

The priest's office shall be theirs for a *perpetual statute*: and thou shalt consecrate Aaron and his sons.... And I will sanctify the tabernacle of the congregation and the altar: I will sanctify also both Aaron and his sons, to minister to me in the priest's office. And I will dwell among the children of Israel, and will be their God. *Exodus* xxix. 9, 44, 45.

And the Lord said unto Aaron.... Therefore thou and thy sons with thee shall keep your priest's office for *every thing of the altar*, and within the vail; and ye shall serve: I have given your priest's office unto you as a service of gift: and *the stranger that cometh nigh shall be put to death*.... Behold, I also have given thee the charge of mine heave offerings of all the hallowed things of the children of Israel; unto thee have I given them *by reason of the anointing*, and to thy sons, *by an ordinance for ever*. *Num.* xviii. 1, 7, 8.

For his zealous vindication of the law, Phinehas the son of Eleazar, the son of Aaron the priest, was thus commended:-

The Lord spake unto Moses, saying, Phinehas...... hath turned my wrath away from the children of Israel, while he was zealous for my sake among them, that I consumed not the children of Israel in my jealousy. Wherefore say, Behold, I give unto him my COVENANT OF PEACE: And he shall have it, and his seed after him, even the covenant of an *everlasting priesthood*; because he was zealous for his God, and made an *atonement* for the children of Israel. *Numbers* xxv. 6-13.

From these texts, two things are evident:-1st, That the priests were the ministers of God for the good of His people, under an everlasting covenant of peace; and 2d, That no "stranger," or person other than a priest, might interfere to do the service which was entrusted to the priesthood, *by reason of the anointing.* [For the anointing and consecration of Aaron and his sons, see *Exodus*, xxviii, xxix.]

The jealousy with which the priest's office was guarded, was shown when Korah and his company, who were Levites, sought the priest' office also, and rose up against Moses and Aaron. They were punished by being swallowed up alive in a pit. *Num.* xvi. For "they shall not come nigh the vessels of the sanctuary and of the altar, that neither they, nor ye [the priests] also die." *Num.* xviii. 2-4.

So, when Saul in his haste, offered a burnt offering, Samuel said to him :-

Thou hast done foolishly: thou hast not kept the commandment of the Lord thy God.... But now thy kingdom shall not continue.... because thou hast not kept that which the Lord commanded thee. 1 *Sam.* xiii.

Again it is recorded of Uzziah, king of Judah :-

When he was strong, his heart was lifted up to his destruction: for he transgressed against the Lord his God, and went into the temple of the Lord to burn incense upon the altar of incense. And Azariah the priest went in after him, and with him fourscore priests..... And they withstood Uzziah the king, and said unto him, It appertaineth not unto thee, Uzziah, to burn incense unto the Lord, but to the priests, the sons of Aaron, that are consecrated to burn incense: go out of the sanctuary; for thou hast trespassed: neither shall it be for thine honour from the Lord God.

Then Uzziah was wroth, and had a censer in his hand to burn incense: and while he was wroth with the priests, the leprosy even rose up in his forehead before the priests in the house of the Lord, from beside the incense altar.... And Uzziah the king was a leper unto the day of his death. 2 *Chron.* xxvi. 16–21.

Malachi thus alludes to the covenant with the priests of the tribe of Levi, and shows what ought to be their character, and what was the nature of their office:–

My covenant was with him [Levi] of *life and peace*; and I gave them to him for the fear wherewith he feared me, and was afraid before my Name. The law of truth was in his mouth, and iniquity was not found in his lips: he walked with me in peace and equity, and *did turn many away from iniquity.* For the priest's lips should keep knowledge, and they should seek the law at his mouth: for he is the *messenger* of the Lord of hosts. *Malachi* ii. 5–7.

Jeremiah speaks of the Jewish priests, and of the Messiah, as both being in the covenant of Noah:–

Thus saith the Lord; David shall never want a man to sit upon the throne of the house of Israel: Neither shall the priests the Levites want a man before me to offer burnt offerings, and to kindle meat offerings, and to do sacrifice continually.... If ye can break my *covenant of the day, and my covenant of the night,* and that there should not be day and night in their season; [the very one made with Noah,] Then may also my covenant be broken with David my servant, that he should not have a Son to reign upon his throne; and with the Levites the *priests, my ministers. Jeremiah* xxxiii. 17–21.

Isaiah shows how the covenant of peace with the priests is mystically joined by the type of the *waters*, to that with the Church over which they minister, whose members are to seek the law at their mouth; and how the Gentiles are also to be in the covenant. He says:—

Thou shalt break forth on the right hand and on the left; and thy seed shall *inherit the Gentiles*, and make the desolate cities to be inhabited.... For thy Maker is thine husband; [The Bride, the Lamb's wife] the Lord of hosts is his name; and thy Redeemer, the Holy One of Israel; The God of the whole earth shall He be called.... For this is as *the waters of Noah* unto me: for as I have sworn that the waters of Noah should no more go over the earth; so have I sworn that I would not be wroth with thee, nor rebuke thee. For the mountains shall depart, and the hills be removed; but my kindness shall not depart from thee, neither shall the *covenant of my peace* be removed, saith the Lord that hath mercy on thee. *Isaiah* liv. 3–10.

St. Peter explains the mystical meaning of the Ark, and the waters:—

The longsuffering of God waited in the days of Noah while the ark was a preparing, wherein few, that is, eight souls were saved by water. The like figure whereunto, even *baptism*, doth also now save us (not the putting away of the filth of the flesh, but the answer of a good conscience toward God,) by the resurrection of Jesus Christ. 1 *Peter* iii. 20, 21.

THE NEW PRIESTHOOD.

In the process of time, the priests became lax and corrupt, as we learn from Malachi:—

Ye are departed out of the way; ye have caused many to stumble at the law; ye have corrupted the covenant of Levi, saith the Lord of hosts. Therefore have I also made you contemptible and base before all the people, according as ye have not kept my ways, but have been partial in the law. *Malachi* ii. 8, 9.

Because of the corrupt practices into which the priests of the tribe of Levi had fallen, and the imperfection of their ministry, as adapted to a more advanced age, God established a new order of the priesthood. He did not suffer the *office* to expire, for He had promised that it should be everlasting.

Think not that I am come to destroy the Law, or the Prophets: I am not come to destroy, but to fulfil.

Thus saith our Lord Jesus Christ. *Matt.* v. 17.

His covenant with David, that he should have a son to reign upon his throne, was accomplished when the Angel announced:—

Behold, I bring you good tidings of great joy, which shall be to all people. For unto you is born this day in the city of David a Saviour, which is Christ the Lord. *Luke* ii. 10, 11.

Then, with the Angel, a multitude of the heavenly host proclaimed anew the *Covenant of His peace*, saying:—

Glory to God in the highest, and on earth peace, good will toward men. *Luke* ii. 14.

The covenant with the priests was perfected in Him who was the promised Messiah; who, while declaring that He was a King, yet said:—

My kingdom is not of this world. *John* xviii. 36, 37.

For every High Priest taken from among men is *ordained* for men in things pertaining to God, that he may offer both gifts and sacrifices for sins..... And no man *taketh this honour unto himself*, but he that is called of God, as was Aaron. So also Christ glorified not Himself to be made an High Priest; but He that said unto Him, Thou art my Son, to day have I begotten thee. As He saith also in another place, [*Ps.* cx. 4] Thou art a Priest for ever after the order of Melchisedec. *Hebrews* v. 1-6.

St. Paul, himself a Jew, thus explains to the Jews the consequence of the corrupt state of their priests, to which Malachi referred:—

If perfection were by the Levitical priesthood, (for under it the people received the law,) what further need was there that another priest should rise after the order of Melchisedec, and not be called after the order of Aaron?.... For it is evident that our Lord sprang out of Juda; of which tribe Moses spake nothing concerning priesthood.... There is verily a disannulling of the commandment going before for the weakness and unprofitableness thereof. For the law made nothing perfect, but the bringing in of a better hope did; by the which we draw nigh unto God...... And they truly were many Priests, because they were not suffered to continue by reason of death: But this man, because He continueth ever, hath an unchangeable priesthood...... Such an High Priest became us, who is holy, harmless, undefiled, separate from sinners, and made higher than the heavens. *Heb.* vii. 11-28.

The Messiah, the Son of God, promised in the covenant with David, could alone perfectly fulfil the condition of holiness in a High Priest. All of the four Evangelists describe the visible anointing of this High Priest, by the descent of the Holy Spirit upon Him at the time of His baptism; and St. John bears this testimony in that connection:—

He that sent me to baptize with water, the same said unto me, Upon whom thou shalt see the Spirit descending, and remaining on Him, the same is He which baptizeth with the Holy Ghost. *John* i. 29-34.

He says of Himself:-

The Spirit of the Lord is upon me, because He hath *anointed* me to preach the Gospel to the poor. *Luke* iv. 18-21.

And St. Peter says of Him:-

How God *anointed* Jesus of Nazareth with the Holy Ghost and with power. *Acts* x. 38.

And this is the work of His office:-

Christ [which means *anointed,*] is not entered into the holy places made with hands, which are the *figures of the true*; but into heaven itself, now to appear in the presence of God *for us*.... Now once in the end of the world hath He appeared to put away sin by the sacrifice of *Himself*. *Hebrews* ix. 24, 26.

For it is not possible that the blood of bulls and of goats should take away sins.... He taketh away the first, [*covenant*] that He may establish the second..... For by one offering [of Himself,] He hath perfected for ever them that are sanctified. *Heb.* x. 4-14.

The first covenant, which required the shedding of the blood of animals in atonement for sin, was a type of the second, which was perfected by the blood of Jesus Christ. The first was taken away by Him when He fulfilled the type "by the sacrifice of Himself."

Now this great High Priest called and ordained twelve Apostles, whom he sent to "preach, saying, The kingdom of heaven is at hand." *Matt.* x. 7.

After these things the Lord appointed other *seventy* also, and sent them two and two before His face into every city and place, whither He Himself would come. *Luke* x. 1.

This is analogous to the seventy elders whom the Lord commanded Moses to appoint.

The Apostles were *anointed* to their office by the descent of the Holy Ghost upon them on the day of Pentecost. (*Acts* ii. 1-4.) The character of the New Dispensation is here indicated: It is a *Spiritual*, not a carnal one. The anointing oil was only a type of the consecration by the Holy Spirit.

These anointed Apostles forthwith proceeded to exercise their ministry; and we read that:-

The same day there were added unto them about three thousand souls.... And the Lord added to the Church daily such as should be saved. *Acts* ii. 41, 47.

Thus was laid, first, the foundation of the Priesthood of the Second Covenant; and then, by them, of the Christian Church.

Before His ascent up to heaven, Christ gave to His Apostles this commission:-

Go ye therefore, and teach all nations, *baptizing* them in the Name of the Father, and of the Son, and of the Holy Ghost: Teaching them to observe all things whatsoever I have commanded you: and, lo, I am with you *alway, even unto the end of the world*. *Matthew* xxviii. 19, 20.

Here again is the mystical connection of the Priesthood and the Church by *water*, which in baptism is the *token* of the New Covenant. For:-

Except a man be born of *water* and of the Spirit, he cannot enter into the kingdom of God. *John* iii. 5.

He that believeth and is baptized shall be saved. *Mark* xvi. 16.

Water is the token of the Covenant of peace, foreshadowed by the *Rainbow*, and taking the place of the bloody rite, circumcision; for the blood of Christ was shed once for all. Heb. x. 10, 12.

As the Lord's covenant with the priests the Levites, was *to continue for ever*, so He who abideth a High Priest for ever, promised to be with His ministers *alway even unto the end of the world*. Is it not right, then, that this Christian Priesthood should, after the example of the Jewish, be carefully guarded? The Church does what she can to this end. The twenty third of the Articles of Religion, in the Book of Common Prayer, says:—

It is not lawful for any man to take upon him the office of public preaching or ministering the Sacraments in the Congregation, before he be lawfully called, and sent to execute the same. And those we ought to judge lawfully called and sent which be chosen and called to this work by men who have public authority given unto them in the Congregation, to call and send Ministers into the Lord's Vineyard.

THE CHURCH.

St. John saw "The holy city, New Jerusalem, coming down from God, out of heaven, prepared as a bride adorned for her husband." This is the *Bride the Lamb's wife.* (*Rev.* xxi. 2, 9.) It is the Church of Christ, of which St. Paul says:—

The husband is the head of the wife, even as Christ is the head of the Church: and He is the Saviour of the body. *Ephesians* v. 23.

It is the fulfilment of the covenant which Isaiah predicted to her whose *Maker is her husband*; from whom His *Covenant of peace* shall not be removed; and whose seed shall inherit the Gentiles.

The members of this Church are all those who :—

Have put on the new man, which is renewed in knowledge after the image of Him that created him: Where there is neither Greek nor Jew, circumcision nor uncircumcision, Barbarian, Scythian, bond nor free: but Christ is all, and in all. *Col.* iii. 10, 11.

We have seen the Church of Israel, and the Church of Christ, both of them established under a COVENANT OF PEACE, made with them through their *Priesthood*, which is to be perpetual. But they must be seen united together under the BOW of promise, and under the same High Priest who "ever liveth to make intercession for them."(*Heb.* vii. 25.) Because :—

God hath not cast away His people [Israel] which He foreknew.... But rather through their fall salvation is come unto the Gentiles, for to provoke them to jealousy.... And they also, if they abide not still in unbelief, shall be graffed in: for God is able to graff them in again.... Blindness in part is happened to Israel, until the fulness of the Gentiles be come in. And so all Israel shall be saved: as it is written, [*Is.* lix. 20, 21.–*Jer.* xxxi. 31–33.] There shall come out of Sion the Deliverer, and shall turn away ungodliness from Jacob: for this is my *covenant* unto them, when I shall take away their sins. *Rom.* xi. 2–27.

Here is the vision which Ezekiel saw of the great High Priest sitting upon His throne, and the RAINBOW round about it :—

Above the firmament that was over their heads was the likeness of a throne, as the appearance of a *sapphire stone*: and upon the likeness of the throne was the likeness as the appearance of a Man above upon it... As the appearance of the BOW *that is in the cloud in the day of rain*, so was the appearance of the brightness round about. This was the appearance of the likeness of the glory of the Lord. *Ezek.* i. 26-28.

And here is St. John's vision:—

Immediately I was in the Spirit: and, behold, a throne was set in heaven, and One sat on the throne. And He that sat was to look upon like a *jasper* and a *sardine stone*: and there was a RAINBOW round about the throne, in sight like unto an *emerald*. And round about the throne were four and twenty seats: and upon the seats I saw four and twenty elders sitting, clothed in white raiment; and they had on their heads crowns of gold. And out of the throne proceeded lightnings and thunderings and voices. *Rev.* iv. 2-5.

Jesus said to His disciples:—

Ye which have followed me, in the regeneration when the Son of man shall sit in the throne of His glory, ye also shall sit upon twelve thrones, judging the twelve tribes of Israel. *Matt.* xix. 28.

The worship round the throne is thus described:—

I beheld, and I heard the voice of many angels round about the throne.... Saying with a loud voice, Worthy is the Lamb that was slain to receive power, and riches, and wisdom, and strength, and honour, and glory, and blessing. And every creature which is in heaven, and on the earth, and under the earth, and such as are in the sea, and all that are in them, heard I saying, Blessing, and honour, and glory, and power, be unto Him that sitteth upon the throne, and unto the Lamb for ever and ever. *Rev.* v. 11-14.

There is a remarkable prediction of all this by David, "the Sweet Psalmist of Israel":—

The Lord hath sworn in truth unto David; He will not turn from it; Of the fruit of thy body will I set upon thy throne. If thy children will keep my *Covenant* and my testimony that I shall teach them, their children shall also sit upon thy throne for evermore. For the Lord hath chosen Zion; He hath desired it for His habitation. This is my rest for ever: here will I dwell; for I have desired it. I will abundantly bless her provision: I will satisfy her poor with bread. I will also clothe her priests with salvation: and her saints shall shout aloud for joy. There will I make the horn of David to bud: I have ordained a lamp for mine anointed. His enemies will I clothe with shame: but upon Himself shall His crown flourish. *Ps.* cxxxii. 11-18.

THE SIGNIFICANCE OF THE COLOURS.

There are gorgeous hues in this Covenant of Peace, which the imagination of man can hardly comprehend. Let us try to get a glimpse of the significance of those lustrous colors which belong to the *token* of the Covenant, and also to the foundation stones of the walls of the Holy City of Him who sitteth upon the throne which is therein. Reason, or fancy, may find an application of the description to the experiences of a Christian's life.

The seven colors of the RAINBOW, are *red*, the outermost, orange, yellow, green, blue, indigo, and *violet* the innermost. It is remarkable that these correspond with the colors of the twelve stones which are described as composing the foundation of the walls of the Holy City. *Rev.* xxi. 10-27.

"The first foundation was Jasper": *crimson*, the outer color of the rainbow; the color of suffering; signifying the Passion of the Lord, and the crucial trials through which His brethren pass to His eternal rest in heaven.

"The second, Sapphire:" *blue*, the color of "truth and calmness." "The deep blue of the clearest and most cloudless heaven." When Moses, Aaron, and the Elders, went up to meet the Lord on Mount Sinai, they saw:—
The God of Israel: and there was under His feet as it were a paved work of a *sapphire stone*, and as it were the body of heaven in his clearness. *Ex.* xxiv. 10.

"The third, a Chalcedony:" pure, lustrous, pearl *white*, signifying purity, humility, light.

"The fourth, an Emerald:" deep *green*, refreshing and grateful, like the fresh grass and foliage. The emblem of Hope.

"The fifth, Sardonyx:" a combination of sardius and chalcedony; *red*, with stripes of pearl *white*. The red is emblem of that tender love which endured all agony, even to its precious blood-shedding; and the intermingled white, of the purity which comes of patient suffering for the Lord's sake.

"The sixth, Sardius:" *red*. This is the middle stone, and an emblem of that divine love, that charity—the greatest of all—which binds in one, the "lively stones" of the Church. 1 *Pet.* ii. 5.

"The seventh, Chrysolite:" *yellow green*, clear and transparent; hope, tinged with pure, refined gold. The emblem of the soul purified from the dross of sin in the fire of affliction.

"The eighth, Beryl:" *pale blue*; an emblem of peaceful rest.

"The ninth, Topaz:" *yellow*, suggesting the illuminating flashes of the Spirit, like the sun's rays, revealing the goodness of God.

"The tenth, Chrysopiasus:" bright *bluish-green*; the hope of heaven.

"The eleventh, Jacinth:" *purple*; an emblem of the Royal Priesthood. 1 *Peter* ii. 9.

"The twelfth, Amethyst:" This is the last stone; Of *violet*, the inner color of the Rainbow; a mingling of the heavenly rest *blue*, and the *red* of the Lord's passion and love.

God prescribed for the High Priest "Holy garments.... for glory and for beauty," in which the blue, the purple, and the scarlet colors were conspicuous. *Ex.* xxviii. 1-12. Then there was the "Breastplate of judgment," with the same colors. In it were four rows of stones, three in a row:—

The first row shall be a sardius, a topaz, a carbuncle.... The second row.... an emerald, a sapphire, and a diamond. The third row, a ligure, an agate, and an amethyst. And the fourth row, a beryl and an onyx, and a jasper: they shall be set in gold. *Ex.* xxviii. 15.

These beautiful symbols illustrate St. Paul's encouraging words to the Church, in which he so specifically refers to the three Holy Persons, Father, Son, and Spirit:—

Now in Christ Jesus ye who sometimes were far off are made nigh by the blood of Christ.... For through Him we both have access by one Spirit unto the Father. Now therefore ye are no more strangers and foreigners, but fellowcitizens with the saints, and of the household of God; and are built upon the foundation of the Apostles and Prophets, Jesus Christ Himself being the Chief Corner Stone; in whom all the building fitly framed together groweth unto an holy temple in the Lord: In whom ye also are builded together for an habitation of God through the Spirit. *Eph.* ii. 13.

They also seem to show something of the meaning of St. John's vision of Him who sat upon the throne. He was to look upon like a jasper and a sardine stone; picturing His suffering for love of His Church. The token of His Covenant of peace seen round about His throne, was Hope realized. The four and twenty Elders, were the twelve fathers on whom His chosen Church of Israel was founded, now one with that of His twelve Apostles. They were clothed with the white robes of fine linen—"the righteousness of saints." (*Rev.* xix. 8.) Hence the *surplice*, emblem of the purity of the priestly office. Before His throne burned for ever, the "seven lamps of fire.... which are the Seven Spirits of God, (*Rev.* iv. 5.) the fire of the Holy Spirit of Love unlimited, unsurpassed.

Of this Holy City, the Church thus sings:—

>With jasper glow thy bulwarks,
>   Thy streets with emeralds blaze;
>The sardius and the topaz
>   Unite in thee their rays;
>Thine ageless walls are bonded
>   With amethyst unpriced;
>The Saints build up its fabric,
>   And the corner-stone is Christ.
>   *Hymn* 492.

And thus the Church teaches us to pray:—

O ALMIGHTY God, who hast built thy Church upon the foundation of the Apostles and prophets, Jesus Christ Himself being the head cornerstone; grant us so to be joined together in unity of spirit by their doctrine, that we may be made an holy temple acceptable unto thee, through Jesus Christ our Lord. Amen. *Collect for St. Simon and St. Jude, Apostles.*

CHAPTER III.

TYPES OF THE ATONEMENT.

———:o:———

A type is defined to be, That by which something future is prefigured. And Archbishop Tillotson says, "The Apostle shows the Christian religion to be in truth and substance what the Jewish was only in type and shadow."

As, through the blended prismatic colors of the rainbow, the true LIGHT is revealed, so, through the types of the Bible stories, is seen more clearly

> The Light that has no evening,
> That knows nor moon nor sun,
> The Light so new and golden,
> The Light that is but one.

ABEL'S OFFERING.

Of the two sons of Adam we read:—

Abel was a keeper of sheep, but Cain was a tiller of the ground. And in process of time it came to pass, that Cain brought of the fruit of the ground an offering unto the Lord. And Abel, he also brought of the firstlings of his flock, and of the fat thereof. And the Lord had respect unto Abel and to his offering: But unto Cain and to his offering, He had not respect. And Cain was very wroth. *Gen.* iv. 2–5.

St. Paul says:—

By *faith* Abel offered unto God a more excellent sacrifice than Cain, by which he obtained witness that he was righteous, God testifying of his gifts. *Heb.* xi. 4.

It thus appears that the principle, "It is the *blood* that maketh an atonement for the soul," (*Levit.* xvii. 11.) was revealed to Abel through faith. His choice of the *firstlings*, shows how clear was the revelation to him of the firstborn Son of God as the real atonement.

And the Lord said unto Cain.... If thou doest not well, sin [that is, properly translated, *a sin-offering*] lieth at the door. *Genesis* iv. 7.

The meaning is, If thou dost commit sin, the proper atonement in the form of a lamb, lies, or crouches, at your very door, as the lambs in that pastoral country were wont to do. Cain's offering "of the fruit of the ground," was rejected because he had not faith to perceive the true significance of sacrifice.

Of the real atonement for our souls, typefied by Abel's lamb, St. John says:—

I heard a loud voice saying in heaven, Now is come salvation, and strength, and the kingdom of our God, and the power of His Christ: for the accuser of our brethren is cast down, which accused them before our God day and night. And they overcame him by the BLOOD OF THE LAMB, and by the word of their testimony. *Revelation* xii. 10, 11.

This is the true faith.

ISAAC.

When Abram was ninety years old and nine, the Lord appeared to Abram, and said unto him, I Am the Almighty GOD; walk before me, and be thou perfect. And I will make my covenant between me and thee, and will multiply thee exceedingly.... Neither shall thy name any more be called Abram, but thy name shall be Abraham [which means, *Father of a great nation*]; for a father of many nations have I made thee...... And God said, Sarah thy wife shall bear thee a son indeed; and thou shalt call his name Isaac: and I will establish my covenant with him for an everlasting covenant, and with his seed after him. *Genesis* xvii. 1-19.

Abraham was an hundred years old, when his son Isaac was born unto him. And God said unto Abraham... in Isaac shall thy seed be called. *Gen.* xxi. 5-12

After these things, God did tempt Abraham...... And He said, Take now thy son, thine *only son* Isaac, whom *thou lovest,* and get thee into the land of Moriah; and offer him there for a burnt offering upon one of the mountains which I will tell thee of...... Then on *the third day* Abraham lifted up his eyes, and saw the place afar off.... And Abraham took the wood of the burnt offering, and *laid it upon Isaac his son*; and he took the fire in his hand, and a knife; and they went both of them together. And Isaac spake unto Abraham his father, and said, My father.... Behold the fire and the wood: but where is the lamb for a burnt offering? And Abraham said, My son, *God will provide Himself a lamb* for a burnt offering. *Gen.* xxii. 1-8.

And the Angel of the Lord called unto him out of heaven and said.... Lay not thine hand upon the lad... for now I know that thou fearest God, seeing thou hast not withheld thy son, thine only son from me.... In thy seed shall all the nations of the earth be blessed; because thou hast obeyed my voice. *Gen.* xxii. 11-18.

Here is an evident type of what St. John says:—

God so loved the world, that He gave His *only begotten Son,* that whosoever believeth in Him should not perish, but have everlasting life. *John* iii. 16.

Twice was a voice heard from heaven, saying. "*This is my beloved Son.*" The first time was when Jesus was baptized in Jordan. (*Matt.* iii. 13-17.) The second time was when Jesus was transfigured on the mountain. (*Luke* ix. 28-35.) And it agrees with what David the prophet says :—

Yet have I set [or, *anointed*] my king upon my holy hill of Zion. I will declare the decree: the Lord hath said unto me, Thou art my Son; this day have I begotten thee. *Psalm* ii. 6, 7.

There are other parts of the type, pointing to the Lamb whom God would provide, and of whom St. John testifies:—

Behold the Lamb of God which taketh away the sin of the world. *John* i. 29.

The temple at Jerusalem was built on Mount Moriah, which was doubtless in the land of Moriah to which Abraham was directed to go. There were many hills, or mountains, in the neighbourhood, and, as Scott says, there is no improbability in the general opinion, that the one which God told Abraham of, was Mount Calvary, where Christ, the great Anti-type, was afterwards crucified; and that it was selected with reference to that event.

Isaac bore the wood for the burnt offering; so:—

Jesus *bearing His cross* went forth into a place called the place of a skull, which is called in the Hebrew Golgotha: where they crucified Him. *John* xix. 17, 18.

It is a curious coincidence, to say the least, that the words, "The third day," should occur in the narrative of Abraham's journey with Isaac, and in that too of the resurrection from the dead of our Lord: Whom they slew, and hanged on a tree.

Him God raised up *the third day.* Acts x. 39, 40.

In allusion to the Angel's promise to Abraham St. Paul says:

To Abraham and his Seed were the promises made. He saith not, And to seeds, as of many; but as of one, And to thy Seed, which is Christ. (*Gal.* iii. 16.) For verily He took not on Him the nature of angels; but He took on Him the seed of Abraham. Heb. ii. 16.

David prophesies of Messiah:—

My flesh also shall rest in hope. For thou wilt not leave my soul in hell; neither wilt thou suffer thine Holy One to see corruption. (*Ps.* xvi. 9, 10.) For David speaketh concerning Him...... being a prophet, and knowing that God had sworn with an oath to him, that of the fruit of his loins, according to the flesh, He would raise up Christ to sit on his throne; He seeing this before spake of the resurrection of Christ, that His soul was not left in hell, neither His flesh did see corruption. *Acts* ii. 26–31.

And St. Paul thus applies the type:—

By faith Abraham, when he was tried, offered up Isaac: and he that had received the promises offered up his only begotten son, of whom it was said, That in Isaac shall thy seed be called: accounting that God was able to raise him up, even from the dead; from whence also he received him in a *figure.* Heb. xi. 17-19.

The Lord promised Abraham:—

I will multiply thy seed as the stars of the heaven, and as the sand which is upon the sea shore; and thy seed shall possess the gate of his enemies. *Gen.* xxii. 17.

When the children of Israel had become very numerous, and were oppressed in Egypt, the Lord commanded Moses:—

Thou shalt say unto Pharaoh, Thus saith the Lord,

Israel is my *Son*, even my *Firstborn*.... Let my Son go, that he may serve me. *Exodus* iv. 22, 23.

While pondering the singular fact of Abraham's exceeding old age when his son was born, and the wonderful history of that great and powerful nation which descended from him, and which God called His firstborn son, the vision of Daniel seems to come to our aid to explain, if we could but comprehend it, the grandest type in the story of Isaac:

I saw in the night visions, and, behold, One like the SON OF MAN came with the clouds of heaven, and came to the ANCIENT OF DAYS, and they brought Him near before Him. And there was given Him dominion, and glory, and a kingdom, that all people, nations, and languages, should serve Him: His dominion is an everlasting dominion, which shall not pass away, and His kingdom that which shall not be destroyed. *Daniel* vii. 13, 14.

They who cavil at the mystery of the divine Sonship of Christ because they cannot understand it, would do well to heed what the Lord said to Abraham when Sarah laughed within herself, doubting that the promise to her of a son could be fulfilled:—

Is any thing too hard for the Lord? *Gen.* xviii. 14.

JOSEPH.

We read of Joseph that his brethren cast him into a *pit*: and the pit was empty, there was *no water* in it. He was afterward drawn up from the pit, and sold to the Ishmaelites for twenty pieces of silver. (*Gen.* xxxvii. 24) And God sent him into Egypt to save life, by distributing bread. *Gen.* xlv. 5.

Joseph typifies:—1st, What Zechariah says:—

As for thee also, by the *blood of thy covenant* I have sent forth thy prisoners out of the *pit* wherein is *no water.* Zechariah ix. 11.

2d, What our Lord Jesus says:—

For as Jonas was three days and three nights in the whale's belly; so shall the Son of man be three days and three nights in the heart of the earth. [*the pit.*] *Matthew* xii. 40.

Jesus here applies the significant type of Jonah to Himself. *Jonah* i, ii.

3d, What St. Paul says:—

The God of peace, that brought again from the dead our Lord Jesus, that great Shepherd of the sheep, through the blood of the everlasting covenant. *Heb.* xiii. 20.—*Isaiah* xii. 6, 7.

4th, What Jeremiah says:—

The BREATH of our nostrils, the ANOINTED of the Lord, was taken in their *pits*, of whom we said, Under His shadow we shall live among the heathen. *Lam.* iv. 20.

5th, The betrayal of Jesus for thirty pieces of silver, (*Matt.* xxvi. 15.) which was predicted by Zechariah 500 years before:—

So they weighed for my price thirty pieces of silver. *Zechariah* xi. 12.

6th, Joseph was thrown into prison in Egypt with two malefactors, the chief butler and the chief baker. So Jesus was crucified between two thieves, in fulfilment of the prophecy:—

He was numbered with the transgressors. *Is.* liii. 12.

To make the type of Joseph complete as to the *blood*, we must note that his brethren killed a kid, often called a lamb, and dipped his coat of many colors in the *blood*, by the side of the *pit*; (*Gen.* xxxvii. 31.) As if to foreshadow Him who said:—

I will tread them in mine anger, and trample them in my fury; and their blood shall be sprinkled upon my garments, and I will stain all my raiment. *Is.* lxiii. 3.

And of whom it is said:—

He was clothed with a vesture dipped in blood: and His name is called THE WORD OF GOD. *Rev.* xix. 13.

The coat of many colors was a mark of distinction, indicating heirship in the one on whom it was bestowed. Joseph's coat has been supposed to symbolize the Church in all its varied forms, which is sanctified by the sprinkling of the blood of the covenant. It may also typify the "robe of righteousness," which when it envelopes a man, gives him comfort, and protection from the storms of sin and trouble; and which, dipped in the blood of the Lamb, raises him out of the pit to an everlasting inheritance.

After Joseph had been raised from the pit, and was set over all the land of Egypt by Pharaoh, (*Gen.* xli. 41.) his father and his brethren, the progenitors of the house of Israel, came and lived under *his shadow* among the *heathen* Egyptians.

David promises as a reward to the righteous:—

He that dwelleth in the secret place of the Most High, shall abide under the *shadow* of the Almighty... He shall cover thee with His feathers, and under His wings shalt thou trust. *Psalm* xci. 1, 4.

And the Lord Jesus said:—

O Jerusalem, Jerusalem, thou that killest the prophets, and stonest them which are sent unto thee, how often would I have gathered thy children together, even as a hen gathereth her chickens under her wings, and ye would not! *Matt.* xxiii. 37.

Jesus is shown to be the ANOINTED of the Lord

by the prophecy of David:—

The kings of the earth set themselves, and the rulers take counsel together, against the Lord, and against His *Anointed*. *Psalm* ii. 2.

The company of disciples thus quoted this:—

The kings of the earth stood up, and the rulers were gathered together against the Lord, and against His CHRIST.... For of a truth, [said they] against thy Holy Child Jesus, whom thou hast *anointed*, both Herod, and Pontius Pilate, with the Gentiles, and the people of Israel, were gathered together. *Acts* iv. 26, 27.

The dreams of the chief butler and the chief baker are remarkable. The chief butler saw a *vine* with three branches. [I am the true vine. *John* xv. 1.] The three branches were three days, at expiration of which the butler was raised to his place; [the third day Christ rose from the dead,] and again pressed *wine* in his cup for the king. The chief baker saw three baskets filled with bread, or bakemeats, upon his head; and the birds did eat them out of the basket upon his head. The three baskets were the three days at expiration of which he was hanged on a *tree*. (*Gen*. xl.) As Joseph predicted pardon to one offender, while the other was left to punishment, so Jesus said to the penitent thief: "To day shalt thou be with me in paradise." (*Luke* xxiii. 43.) The fruit of the vine and the baker's bread, are the elements through receiving of which in faith, those who abide in Him who is the true *vine*, shall be raised to their place at His right hand; while they who abide not in Him shall be condemned; and they, as it were, shall hang on a tree.

THE SCAPEGOAT.

One ordinance of the Levitical law, in respect to the great day of atonement, when expiation was made for the sins of the people, was that the priest should cast lots on two goats which he presented before the Lord at the door of the Tabernacle; one lot for the Lord, and the other for the *scapegoat*. The priest offered the one upon which the Lord's lot fell for a sin offering. Then he laid both his hands upon the head of the live goat, and confessed over him all the iniquities of the Children of Israel:—
And the goat shall bear upon him all their iniquities unto a land not inhabited; and he shall let go the goat in the wilderness. *Levit.* xvi.

A similar type of the Lord's death and resurrection is shown by the two birds, in "the law of the leper in the day of his cleansing". *Levit.* xiv. 2–7.

When Abraham was restrained by the angel, from offering up Isaac:—
Abraham lifted up his eyes, and looked, and behold behind him a ram caught in a thicket by his horns: and Abraham went and took the ram, and offered him up for a burnt offering in the stead of his son. *Gen.* xxii.

Here the ram was the typical sin offering, and Isaac the scapegoat.

When He "that loved us, and washed us from our sins in His own blood"; (*Rev.* i. 5, 6.) "Who His own self bare our sins in His own body on the tree, that we, being dead to sins, should live unto righteousness"; (1 *Peter* ii. 24.) was betrayed and led away to trial:—
There followed Him a certain young man, having a

linen cloth cast about his naked body; and the young men laid hold on him: and he left the linen cloth, and fled from them naked. *Mark* xiv.51, 52.

The Rev. Henry Melville's idea is that, While here Jesus was the true sin offering, the young man in the linen cloth represented the *scapegoat*. This young man was clad in the garment called *sindon*. It would seem that he was a devotee who wore this garment as a mark of his religious fervour, which may account for the desire of the infuriated Jews to seize him. But the sindon was also a garment like a shroud, in which the dead were enveloped, and in this lies the type. Nothing more is heard of the young man after his escape, than of the goat let go in the wilderness. So He who bare our sins ascended out of sight to His place in heaven. As the young man, escaping from the fierce multitude which sought to detain him, left behind his linen cloth, the habiliment of the grave, so the Lord, rising from the dead in spite of His enemies, left the linen clothes in which His body was enveloped, "laid by themselves" in the tomb.

Again, the type appears when Pilate said:—
Ye have a custom, that I should release unto you one at the Passover: will ye therefore that I release unto you the King of the Jews? Then cried they all again, saying, Not this man, but Barabas. *John* xviii. 39, 40.

In the types two are required to show forth the atonement and the resurrection. In the fulfilment it required only the one Divine Being.

THE BLOOD OFFERING.

According to the principle "It is the blood that maketh an atonement for the soul," the Law required that the priest, having killed the beast for a sin offering, should sprinkle its blood around the altar; and that the body be carried forth and burned without the camp. *Levit.* xvi. 27. In allusion to this St. Paul says:—

The bodies of those beasts, whose blood is brought into the sanctuary by the High Priest for sin, are burned without the camp. Wherefore Jesus also, that He might sanctify the people with His own blood, suffered *without the gate. Heb.* xiii. 11, 12.—He bearing His cross went forth into a place called the place of a skull ....where they crucified Him. *John* xix. 16-18.

How is all the type fulfilled, since His blood was not brought into the sanctuary and sprinkled on the altar, but was shed outside the city?

The sprinkling with blood was the old testament. But:—

Christ being come an high priest of good things to come.... Neither by the blood of goats and calves, but by His own blood He entered in *once* into the holy place, having obtained eternal redemption for us..... And for this cause He is the Mediator of the new testament.... Nor yet that He should offer Himself *often*, as the High Priest entereth into the holy place every year with blood of others; For then must He often have suffered since the foundation of the world: but now once in the end of the world hath He appeared to put away sin by the sacrifice of Himself. And as it is appointed unto men once to die, but after this the judgment: So Christ was *once* offered to bear the sins of many. *Heb.* ix. 11–28.

We are sanctified through the offering of the body of Jesus Christ once for all...... This man, after He had offered one sacrifice for sins for ever, sat down on the right hand of God...... By one offering He hath perfected for ever them that are sanctified. *Heb.* x. 10–14.

And this is the way they are sanctified:—

Being justified freely by His grace through the redemption that is in Jesus Christ: Whom God hath set forth to be a propitiation *through faith* in His blood, to declare His righteousness for the remission of sins that are past, through the forbearance of God. *Rom.* iii. 24, 25.—St. Paul says in another place:—

The just shall live by faith. *Heb.* x. 38.

So then the type is fulfilled. The blood of the atonement has been shed once for all. Christ having been slain *outside* the city once for ever, "entered in once into the holy place," and is by *faith* spiritually brought into the sanctuary of our souls.

PRACTICAL APPLICATION.

How is the fulfilment of these types to be applied for our benefit?

The first of the sacraments "generally necessary to salvation," is Baptism, in obedience to the Lord's command to His Apostles:—

Go teach all nations, baptizing them in the name of the Father, and of the Son, and of the Holy Ghost. *Matt.* xxviii. 19.

When the Apostles which were at Jerusalem heard that Samaria had received the word of God, they sent unto them Peter and John: Who, when they were come down, prayed for them, that they might receive the Holy Ghost: For as yet He was fallen upon none of them: only they were baptized in the name of the Lord Jesus. Then *laid they their hands on them*, and *they received* the Holy Ghost. *Acts* viii. 14–17.

This is the second step, Confirmation.

St. Paul says to those who have been baptized:–

Your body is the *temple* of the Holy Ghost which is in you, which ye have of God. 1 *Cor.* vi. 19.

And St. Peter says:–

Ye also, as lively stones, are built up a spiritual house, an holy *priesthood*, to offer up spiritual sacrifices, acceptable to God by Jesus Christ. 1 *Pet.* ii. 5.

St. Paul shows what is the proper sacrifice to be offered in this temple, by this priesthood:–

I beseech you therefore, brethren, by the mercies of God, that ye present *your bodies* a living sacrifice, holy, acceptable unto God, which is your reasonable service. *Rom.* xii. 1.

As the priests consecrated by the laying on of hands by the bishop, minister in the sanctuary, baptize, and administer the Lord's Supper, the memorial of the Atonement, so they who have been made by baptism members of the Church of Christ, are, in confirmation consecrated by the laying on of hands by the bishop, to be priests over their own bodies – the temples of the Holy Ghost – to offer up spiritual sacrifices acceptable to God by Jesus Christ. And as a means of grace whereby they obtain strength to live righteously, they are to take the third step, which is to obey the Lord's other command: "This do in remembrance of me," and receive the Communion of the Body and blood of the Lord. This is the other one of the two sacraments.

That they may through faith bring the Lord's body and blood spiritually into their bodies, which are His temple, they are taught in the "Order of Confirmation," as well as in the "Order for the Administration of the Lord's Supper," to use the following prayer:-

O ALMIGHTY Lord, and everlasting God, vouchsafe, we beseech thee, to direct, sanctify, and govern, both our hearts and bodies, in the ways of thy laws, and in the works of thy commandments; that, through thy most mighty protection, both here and ever, we may be preserved in body and soul, through our Lord and Saviour Jesus Christ. *Amen.*

CHAPTER IV.

THE FIRSTBORN—THE FIRSTFRUITS.

———:o:———

Among the many significant types to be found in the holy Scriptures, that of the Firstborn is one of the most obvious and forcible.

Abraham presented his firstborn son to the Lord, and *redeemed* him with a ram which he sacrificed.

When God would redeem Israel from bondage in Egypt, He commanded them, every man, to kill a *lamb without blemish*, and to take of the blood and sprinkle it upon their houses. And the Lord said:-

I will pass through the land of Egypt this night, and will smite all the *firstborn* in the land of Egypt both man and beast.... And when I see the blood, I will pass over you, and the plague shall not be upon you to destroy you. *Exodus* xii. 1–30.

Thus by the sacrifice of the paschal lamb, the *firstborn* of Israel were redeemed from the destruction which fell upon the Egyptians.

And the Lord spake unto Moses, saying, Sanctify unto me all the firstborn.... among the children of Israel, both of man and of beast: it is mine...... Thou shalt set apart unto the Lord.... every firstling that cometh of a beast which thou hast; the males shall be the Lord's.... and all the firstborn of man among thy children shalt thou redeem. *Exodus* xiii. 1–15.

The idea of priesthood connected with the firstborn is shown in the case of the Levites. Instead of the firstborn children of all the tribes, the Lord chose the whole tribe of Levi to be set apart for His special service:—

Thou shalt gather the whole assembly of the Children of Israel together: And thou shalt bring the Levites before the Lord: and Aaron shall offer the Levites for an offering of the Children of Israel, that they may execute the service of the Lord.... And the Levites shall be mine.... For they are wholly given unto me from among the Children of Israel; instead of.... the firstborn of all the children of Israel, have I taken them unto me. For all the firstborn of the children of Israel are mine, both man and beast: on the day that I smote every firstborn in the land of Egypt I sanctified them for myself. And I have taken the Levites for all the firstborn of the children of Israel. *Numbers* viii. 5–18.

The law requires that a man shall acknowledge his firstborn son:—

By giving him a double portion of all that he hath: for he is the beginning of his strength; the right of the firstborn is his. *Deut.* xxi. 15-18.

When Israel called his sons together that he might tell them what should befall them, he said:-
Reuben, thou art my firstborn, my might, and the beginning of my strength, the excellency of dignity, and the excellency of power. *Gen.* xlix. 3.

But there is here a very curious and important apparent exception in the application of the law of primogeniture. Reuben was the eldest son of Israel, yet it was not he in whom the promise was fulfilled, but Judah the youngest son of Jacob by Leah, his first wife. In pronouncing the blessing upon his sons, Jacob passed by Reuben because of the sin which he had committed against his father. So with the next two, Simeon and Levi, of whom he said, "Cursed be their anger, for it was fierce," because of their murder of the Shechemites. But of Judah he said:-
Thou art he whom thy brethren shall praise....Thy father's children shall bow down before thee..... The Sceptre shall not depart from Judah.... until Shiloh come. *Gen.* xxxiv, xlix.

From Judah in process of time sprang Shiloh, the Messiah, in whom all the families of the earth are blessed.

It was Judah (or, Judas, *Matt.* i. 2.) who proposed to save the life of Joseph by selling him to the Midianites for twenty pieces of silver, saying, "What *profit* is it if we slay our brother?" And the consequence was that Joseph went down into Egypt; was numbered with the transgressors, and having, as it were, been resurrected from the pit, became a prince, and saved many lives. So Judas, of the same name, from a motive of cupidity sold the Son of man; and He, going down into the pit, rose again that He might save life. Thus was the law of the firstborn restored through the line of Judah. As St. Paul says:—

For the promise, that he should be the heir of the world, was not to Abraham, or to his seed, *through the Law*, but through *the righteousness of faith. Rom.* iv. 13.

Jehoshaphat, king of Judah, gave his six sons:—

Great gifts of silver, and of gold, and of precious things, with fenced cities in Judah: but the kingdom gave he to Jehoram; because he was the firstborn. 2 *Chron.* xxi. 2, 3.

In all this there is the idea of preference, of sanctity, of being devoted to the Lord, attached to the firstborn. The prophet Micah has a singular allusion:—

Wherewith shall I come before the Lord, and bow myself before the high God? Shall I come before Him with burnt offerings, with calves of a year old? or with ten thousands of rivers of oil? Shall I give my *firstborn for my transgression*, the fruit of my body for the sin of my soul? He hath shewed thee, O man, what is good; and what doth the Lord require of thee, but to do justly, and to love mercy, and to walk humbly with thy God? *Micah* vi. 6–8.

And Zechariah says:—

I will pour upon the house of David, and upon the inhabitants of Jerusalem, the spirit of grace and of supplications: and they shall look upon me whom they have pierced, and they shall mourn for him, as one mourneth for his *only son*, and shall be in bitterness for him, as one that is in bitterness for his *firstborn*.

Zechariah xii. 10.

It would seem that the prophet had in mind the bitter mourning of Pharaoh when:—

The Lord smote all the firstborn in the land of Egypt, from the firstborn of Pharaoh that sat on his throne unto the firstborn of the captive that was in the dungeon. *Exodus* xii. 29.

In the Century Magazine for September 1889, Mr. John A. Paine describes recent discoveries in Egypt which have brought to light the tomb in which the very mummies of this Pharaoh and of his firstborn son were found. The king's name was Mer-en-ptah, signifying "beloved by the god Ptah," anglicised to Menephtah. He had but one child, a son whom he called Seti, because he was "the boon of his tutelary deity, Set—' the giver of life'." And because he was "the sum of his father's joy, the one object of his father's love, he was called Menephtah,—Seti-Menephtah.

Menephtah had become old and inefficient, when the foreigners in Egypt rose in rebellion against him. He led a large army against them, but avoided giving battle, and taking his son with him, retreated up the Nile into Ethiopia. There he remained twelve years. Seti was, at the end of that period, in his eighteenth year. The Egyptians then returned to recover their land. In the conflicts which followed, Seti commanded the Egyptian army, and displayed great personal prowess and masterly generalship. Having subdued the rebels, he became regent, and was regarded as the sure successor to his father's throne. The fearfulness of the visitation upon Pharaoh in the death of this firstborn son, at little over twenty years of age, can now be appreciated. It was this Seti-Menephtah, upon whom alone depended the efficiency of his aged father's throne, and the succession to it.

Zechariah's prophecy connects the Old Testament type with its fulfilment.

The Angel of the Lord appeared unto him in a dream, saying, Joseph, thou son of David, fear not to take unto thee Mary thy wife: for that which is conceived in her is of the Holy Ghost. And she shall bring forth a son, and thou shalt call His name Jesus: for He shall save His people from their sins. Now all this was done, that it might be fulfilled which was spoken of the Lord by the prophet, saying, Behold, a virgin shall.... bring forth a son, and they shall call His name Emmanuel, which being interpreted is, God with us. *Matt.* i. 20-23. - *Isaiah* vii. 14.

And she brought forth her *firstborn* son, and wrapped Him in swaddling clothes, and laid Him in a manger.... And the Angel said unto them, Fear not: for, behold, I bring you good tidings of great joy, which shall be to all people. For unto you is born this day in the city of David a Saviour, which is Christ the Lord.... And when eight days were accomplished for the circumcising of the child, His name was called Jesus, which was so named of the Angel.... And when the days of her purification according to the law of Moses were accomplished, they brought Him to Jerusalem, to present Him to the Lord; (As it is written in the law of the Lord, Every male that openeth the womb shall be called holy to the Lord;) And to offer a sacrifice according to that which is said in the law of the Lord, A pair of turtle doves, or two young pigeons. *Luke* ii. 7-24. - *Levit.* xii.

Thus was this firstborn Son of Mary presented unto God, and redeemed according to the law for the Levitical priesthood. It is remarkable that the Law says of the firstborn of oxen and sheep:-

Seven days it shall be with his dam; on the *eighth* day thou shalt give it to me. *Exodus* xxii. 30.

But of this firstborn Son of the Virgin we are told by St. John:-

I saw the Spirit descending from heaven like a dove, and it abode upon Him.... And I saw, and bare record that this is the Son of God. *John* 1. 32-34.

And Simon Peter answered and said, Thou art the Christ, the Son of the living God. *Matt.* xvi. 16.

Of God St. Paul declares:-

Whom He did foreknow, He did also predestinate to be conformed to the image of His Son, that He might be the *firstborn* among many brethren. *Rom.* viii. 29.— These "brethren" are:-

The general assembly and church of the firstborn, which are written in heaven. *Heb.* xii. 23.— And:-

Jesus is the Mediator of the new covenant, and the blood of sprinkling, that speaketh better things than that of Abel. *Heb.* xii. 24.

St. Paul says:-

The Father.... hath translated us into the kingdom of His dear Son: In whom we have redemption through His blood, even the forgiveness of sins: Who is the image of the invisible God, the firstborn of every creature.... And He is the head of the body, the Church: who is the beginning, the firstborn from the dead. *Col.* i. 12-18.— And St. Peter says:-

Pass the time of your sojourning here in fear: Forasmuch as ye know that ye were not redeemed with corruptible things, as silver and gold, from your vain conversation received by tradition from your fathers; But with the precious blood of Christ, as of a *lamb without blemish* and without spot: who verily was foreordained before the foundation of the world, but was manifest in these last times for you, Who by Him do believe in God, that raised Him up from the dead, and gave Him glory; that your faith and hope might be in God. 1 *Peter* i. 17–21.

Therefore St. Paul says:—

We pray you in Christ's stead, Be ye reconciled to God. For He hath made Him to be sin for us, who knew no sin; that we might be made the righteousness of God in Him. 2 *Cor.* v. 20, 21.

THE PRIESTHOOD OF THE FIRSTBORN.

Some years ago a writer in the Church Journal made some suggestions which, to say the least, are interesting. He says:—

Reasoning from analogy in both the Jewish and Christian dispensations, we infer that there was a divinely appointed priesthood in the antediluvian Church; and it seems probable that the succession lay in the *Firstborn*.

Then he infers from passages of scripture that Cain, the firstborn of Adam, lost his priesthood by want of faith. Again, quoting the passage:—

Seth, to him also there was born a son ...... Enos: then began men to call upon the name of the Lord, (*Gen.* iv. 26.)—the writer says:—

Which whatever it *does* mean, and it is very obscure, certainly *may* mean that the priesthood was vacant from the time of the apostasy of Cain, the firstborn of Adam, till the birth of Enos, the firstborn of Seth.

Of Seth it is said that Adam's wife:—

Bare a son, and called his name Seth: For God, said she, hath appointed me another seed instead of Abel, whom Cain slew. *Gen.* iv. 25.

Is it improbable then that Cain having lost his priesthood through want of faith, and Abel having been slain, the priesthood should be restored through the firstborn of this man Seth, "*appointed*" instead of Abel to whom the priesthood would have been given "through the righteousness of faith?" Perhaps men were then brought by the Priest Enos "to call upon the name of the Lord."

Abram gave tithes to Melchisedec. (*Gen.* xiv. 29.). The supposition that Melchisedec was a patriarchal high priest of the order of the firstborn, may account for his priesthood being above Aaron's, as it is shown to be by what is said of Christ in that connection:—

Thou art a Priest for ever after the order of Melchisedec. *Psalm* cx. 4. – *Heb.* v. 5, 6.

If it be true that there was an interruption in the succession of the priesthood of the firstborn for some time before it fell upon Melchisedec, this may, perhaps, interpret St. Paul's curious designation of him as :—

Without father, without mother, without descent, [or, *pedigree*] having neither beginning of days, nor end of life; [i. e. as to his priesthood] but made like unto the Son of God; [and so His antetype] abideth a Priest continually. *Heb.* vii. 1–3.

It would seem that the Levitical priesthood was taken instead of the firstborn of all the children of Israel, doing away for the time with the priesthood of the firstborn. But the law of the Levitical priesthood was only :—

Added because of transgressions, till the Seed should come, to whom the promise was made. *Gal.* iii.

Christ the firstborn did away with that imperfect law, and restored the priesthood of the firstborn, after the order of Melchisedec, under the law of the Gospel of peace. In this view, St. Paul's declaration becomes more intelligible and forcible :—

Ye are come unto the heavenly Jerusalem, [the true Jerusalem prefigured by the Jewish dispensation] and to the general assembly and church of the firstborn, which are written in heaven. [the true Church of the firstborn Son of God.] *Heb.* xii.

THE FIRSTFRUITS.

As the law dedicated the firstborn of man and beast, the beginning of their strength, their very best, to the service of the Lord; so also it said :—

The first of the *firstfruits* of thy land thou shalt bring into the house of the Lord thy God. *Ex.* xxiii. 19.

And Solomon says :—

Honour the Lord with thy substance, and with the firstfruits of all thine increase: So shall thy barns be filled with plenty, and thy presses shall burst out with new wine. *Prov.* iii. 9, 10.

This is one of the Sentences appointed by the Church to be read at the beginning of Morning Prayer on Thanksgiving Day.

The Prophet Jeremiah says :—

Israel was holiness unto the Lord, and the firstfruits of His increase. *Jer.* ii. 3.

This is the same as the message sent to Pharaoh :—"Israel is my firstborn." *Ex.* iv. 22.

Now, although we know that:—

The whole creation groaneth and travaileth in pain together until now. And not only they, but ourselves also, which have the *firstfruits* of the Spirit, even we ourselves groan within ourselves, waiting for the adoption, to wit, the redemption of our body: (*Rom.* viii. 22, 23.)

Yet, we also know that:—

Now is Christ risen from the dead, and become the firstfruits of them that slept. For since by man came death, by man came also the resurrection of the dead. For as in Adam all die, even so in Christ shall all be made alive. But every man in his own order: Christ the firstfruits; afterward they that are Christ's at His coming. 1 *Cor.* xv. 20-23.

And we know concerning the Father, that:—

Of His own will begat He us with the Word of truth, that we should be a kind of firstfruits of His creatures. *James* i. 18.

Bildad said to Job:—

The light of the wicked shall be put out...... His strength shall be hunger-bitten, and destruction shall be ready at his side. It shall devour the strength of his skin: even the *firstborn of death* shall devour his strength. *Job* xviii. 5, 12, 13.

On this passage Scott remarks:—

The sentence of death pronounced on all mankind, gave birth to diseases; which therefore by a sublime allegory, are styled the offspring of death: and the most horrible disease, that which hath the preeminence in cruelty, is called his firstborn, his might, and the beginning of his strength.

If by sin came disease and death, and the most dreadful of all is the firstborn of death, then how sublime is the idea that the Firstborn Son of God by His death, destroyed both disease and sin of which it was begotten!

Before Him the powerful empire of Pharaoh fell because of disobedience; and his firstborn son on whom rested all his pride and power in his opposition to the Firstborn Son of God, died like the merest captive in the dungeon. So, before Him, that great nation, Israel, whom God had called His firstborn, were scattered like chaff before the wind, because they rejected Him as their King.

The spirit of all this teaching is that, in return for His inestimable gift of His Firstborn Son whom He gave to redeem us from our sins, we should continually offer to our Father our very best. In the words of our Lord, that we should love Him with all our heart, and with all our soul, and with all our strength, and with all our mind; and our neighbour as ourself. (*Luke* x. 27.) And this is the spirit of the Collect for the First Sunday after Easter:—

ALMIGHTY Father, who hast given thine only Son to die for our sins, and to rise again for our justification; grant us so to put away the leaven of malice and wickedness, that we may always serve thee in pureness of living and truth, through the merits of the same thy Son Jesus Christ our Lord. *Amen.*

CHAPTER V.

CIRCUMCISION AND BAPTISM.

————:o:————

The commandment of God to Abraham was:—
This is my covenant, which ye shall keep, between me and you and thy seed after thee; Every man child among you shall be circumcised.... And the uncircumcised man child.... that soul shall be cut off from his people; he hath broken my covenant. *Gen.* xvii. 10, 14.

So when a stranger who sojourned with the Israelites, would eat of the passover, he must first be circumcised, in token that he entered into the covenant by which he would become "as one that is born in the land: for no uncircumcised person shall eat thereof." *Exodus* xii. 48.

Circumcision, then, was the rite to which not only Jews but strangers must submit before they could enjoy the promises given to the Church of Israel.

But even under the Levitical Law, water was used symbolically as a cleansing agent. A leper—leprosy being a type of sin—was cleansed by sprinkling him with water over which a bird had been killed. (*Levit.* xiv. 2-9.) The Levites also were cleansed by sprinkling water of purifying on them. (*Num.* viii. 6, 7.) And unclean persons were purified by sprinkling them with water of separation. (*Numbers* xix.)

Jewish writers say that all male proselytes were required not only to be circumcised, but to be baptized; and that the females were baptized; otherwise they continued to be as Gentiles.

Ezekiel records this message from the Lord:—

I will take you from among the heathen, and gather you out of all countries, and will bring you into your own land. Then will I *sprinkle clean water* upon you, and ye shall be clean: from all your filthiness, and from all your idols, will I cleanse you. A new heart also will I give you, and a new spirit will I put within you: and I will take away the stony heart out of your flesh, and I will give you an heart of flesh. And I will put *my Spirit* within you, and cause you to walk in my statutes, and ye shall keep my judgments, and do them. *Ezek.* xxxvi. 24–27.

In this there seems to be an indication that baptism was to supercede the rite of circumcision.

Our Lord Jesus was obedient to the law of the old Covenant, being circumcised when He was eight days old. (*Luke* ii. 21.) But He came to do away with the covenant of blood in this, as in the oft repeated sacrifice of animals. So He was baptized by St. John in Jordan. (*Matt.* iii. 3–17) And His commission to His Apostles was:— Go teach all nations, *baptizing*-not circumcising-them. And here are our Lord's own words:—

Jesus answered, Verily, verily, I say unto thee, Except a man be born of *water* and of the Spirit, he cannot enter into the kingdom of God. That which is born of the flesh is flesh [the *stony heart* of the flesh]; and that which is born of the Spirit is spirit [*a new heart, and a new spirit*]. Marvel not that I said unto thee, Ye must be born again [that ye must have a new heart, and a new spirit]. The wind bloweth where it listeth, and thou hearest the sound thereof, but canst not tell whence it cometh, and whither it goeth: so is every one that is born of the Spirit. *John* iii. 5–8.

In a Convention, or Council, of the Apostles at Jerusalem, they decided that the Gentiles should no longer be "troubled with words, subverting their souls, saying, Ye must be circumcised, and keep the law;" for they had given no such commandment. *Acts* xv.

And St. Paul says:—

If the uncircumcision keep the righteousness of the law, shall not his uncircumcision be counted for circumcision?.... Neither is that circumcision, which is outward in the flesh: But...... circumcision is that of the heart, in the spirit, and not in the letter; whose praise is not of men, but of God. *Rom.* ii. 26–29.

This would show that circumcision was no longer necessary as the sacrament by which persons are admitted to the Church. But baptism has taken its place; and our Lord's words, "Except a man be born of water and of the Spirit, he cannot enter into the kingdom of God," are equivalent to those of the Law, "The uncircumcised man child shall be cut off from his people."

St. Paul says:—

By one Spirit are we all baptized into one body, whether we be Jews or Gentiles, whether we be bond or free...... For the Body is not one member, but many. 1 *Cor.* xii. 13, 14.—And again:—

God our Saviour.... saved us, by the washing of regeneration, and renewing of the Holy Ghost; which He shed on us abundantly through Jesus Christ our Saviour. *Titus* iii. 4–6.

This is the fulfilment of St. Peter's promise:—

Repent, and be baptized every one of you in the Name of Jesus Christ for the remission of sins, and ye shall receive the gift of the Holy Ghost. *Acts* ii. 38.

St. John the Apostle says:-

This is He that came by water and blood, even Jesus Christ; not by water only, but by water and blood. And it is the Spirit that beareth witness, because the Spirit is truth.... And there are three that bear witness in earth, the Spirit, and the water, and the blood: and these three agree in one. 1 *John* v. 6, 8.

Here as usual we find both the water and the blood together.

When one is about to be baptized, the Minister is instructed to say:-

Dearly beloved, forasmuch as all men are conceived in sin, (and that which is born of the flesh is flesh,)and they who are in the flesh cannot please God, but live in sin, committing many actual transgressions; and our Saviour Christ saith, None can enter the Kingdom of God, except he be regenerate and born anew of water and of the Holy Ghost; I beseech you to call upon God the Father, through our Lord Jesus Christ, that of His bounteous goodness He will grant to this person that which by nature he cannot have; that he may be baptized with water and the Holy Ghost, and received into Christ's holy Church, and be made a lively member of the same.

The Prayer which follows shows the figurative significance of several events in Bible history. By the saving of the just man Noah and his family in the Ark; by the passage of God's chosen people through the waters of the Red Sea-called by St. Paul, their baptism (1 *Cor.* x. 1, 2.)-and by the baptism of the well beloved Son of the Father in the River Jordan, we are taught that the element of water is sanctified to our use in the ark of the

Church, to bring us into its covenant. So that by exercise of the three cardinal virtues, Faith, Hope, Charity, we may pass safely through the waves of this troublesome world, to the land of everlasting life; as did Noah to the land where he offered sacrifice; and as did Israel to their land of promise.

The person is then baptized in the Name of the Father, and of the Son, and of the Holy Ghost; (*Matt.* xxviii. 19.) and thus becomes "fellow citizen with the Saints, and of the household of God."

St. John says that He who hath the Seven Spirits of God saith:—

Him that overcometh will I make a pillar in the temple of my God, and he shall go no more out: and I will write upon him the Name of my God, and the name of the City of my God, which is New Jerusalem, which cometh down out of heaven from my God: and I will write upon him my new Name. *Rev.* iii. 12.

Again He saith, the servants of the Lamb:—

Shall serve Him: And they shall see His face; and His Name shall be written in their foreheads. *Rev.* xxii. 3, 4.—After the baptism:—

Then the Minister shall say: We receive this person into the Congregation of Christ's Flock, and do sign him with the sign of the Cross; (*Here the Minister shall make a Cross upon the person's forehead.*) in token that hereafter he shall not be ashamed to confess the faith of Christ crucified, and manfully to fight under His banner, against sin, the world, and the devil; and to continue Christ's faithful soldier and servant unto his life's end. *Amen.*

The giving of the "Christian Name" and making the sign of the Cross upon the forehead, are fitting emblems of St. John's words.

At the time of the baptism the Minister says the following Prayer:—

ALMIGHTY, everliving God, whose most dearly beloved Son Jesus Christ, for the forgiveness of our sins, did shed out of His most precious side both water and blood; and gave commandment to His disciples, that they should go teach all nations, baptizing them in the name of the Father, and of the Son, and of the Holy Ghost; regard, we beseech thee, the supplications of thy Congregation; sanctify this water to the mystical washing away of sin; and grant that the Person now to be baptized therein may receive the fulness of thy grace, and ever remain in the number of thy faithful children, through Jesus Christ our Lord. *Amen.*

CHAPTER VI.

THE FEASTS—OLD AND NEW.

—:o:—

The Church of Israel was commanded to keep three principal feasts during the year. So the Church now keeps three corresponding spiritual feasts. The command was:—

Three times thou shalt keep a feast unto me in the year. Thou shalt keep the Feast of Unleavened Bread .... in the time appointed of the month Abib; for in it thou camest out from Egypt: and none shall appear before me empty: And the Feast of Harvest, the first fruits of thy labours, which thou hast sown in the field: and the Feast of Ingathering, which is in the end of the year, when thou hast gathered in thy labours out of the field. *Exodus* xxiii. 14-16.

Three times in a year shall all thy males appear before the Lord thy God *in the place which* **He shall choose**; in the Feast of Unleavened Bread, and in the Feast of weeks, and in the Feast of Tabernacles. *Deut.* xvi. 16.—Israel might not keep these feasts anywhere they chose, but in the place which the Lord should choose; for the Lord said:—

Whatsoever man there be of the house of Israel, or of the strangers which sojourn among you, that offereth a burnt offering or sacrifice, And bringeth it not unto the *door of the Tabernacle* of the Congregation, to offer it unto the Lord; even that man shall be cut off from among his people. *Levit.* xvii. 8, 9.

THE PASSOVER — EASTER.

At the time that the plagues were brought upon Egypt, before God would slay the firstborn of the Egyptians, He instituted the Feast of the Passover, for a memorial for ever. (*Exodus* 1-14.) This was a type of the death of the firstborn Son of God; that His blood appearing upon the houses where we are, shall be to us for a token, and the plague shall not be upon us. As St. Paul says:—

In whom we have redemption through His blood even the forgiveness of sins: Who is the image of the invisible God, the firstborn of every creature. *Col.* i. 14, 15.

The Jews used to set apart forty days for extraordinary humiliation before they kept the Passover. After that Jesus was baptized in Jordan:—

He was led up of the Spirit into the wilderness to be tempted of the devil. And when He had fasted forty days and forty nights, He was afterward an hungred.... Then the devil leaveth Him, and, behold, angels came and ministered unto Him. *Matt.* iv. 1–11.

The forty days of Lent which precede Easter, in which "The Church requires such a measure of abstinence as is more especially suited to extraordinary acts and exercises of devotion" (*Table of fasts, Book of Common Prayer*), is analogous to the Jewish fast immediately preceding their Passover; and to our Lord's fasting in the wilderness, before He began His public ministry. This fast is mentioned by Irenæus, who lived only ninety years after the death of St. John the Apostle, as having been observed in and before his time.

The Paschal lamb was to be a male without blemish. *Ex.* xii. 5.–"Ye shall not offer unto the Lord that which is bruised, or crushed, or broken or cut." *Levit.* xxii. 24. Not a bone of it should be broken. *Ex.* xii. 46. Nothing should remain of it, – to see corruption–but that which remained should be burned. *Ex.* xii. 10. And a bunch of *hyssop* should be dipped in its blood, with which the door should be sprinkled. *Ex.* xii. 22.

These were all types. St. Peter says, We are redeemed "with the precious blood of Christ, as of a lamb without blemish and without spot." 1 *Pet.* i. 18, 19. When those who crucified the Lord Jesus came to Him, "and saw that He was dead already, they brake not His legs.... that the scripture should be fulfilled, A bone of Him shall not be broken." *John* xix. 33, 36 – *Ps.* xxxiv. 20. David "spake of the resurrection of Christ, that His soul was not left in hell, neither His flesh did see corruption." *Acts* ii. 31 – *Ps.* xvi. 10. When the

Lord Jesus upon the cross saith, I thirst, "they filled a spunge with vinegar, and put it upon *hyssop*, and put it to His mouth." *John* xix. 28, 29. It is also remarkable that Jesus made His last entry into Jerusalem on the first day of the week, at the very time that the flocks of lambs for the sacrifice were driven through the gates.

In the Gospel according to St. Luke we read :—

Now the feast of Unleavened Bread drew nigh, which is called The Passover. And the Chief Priests and Scribes sought how they might kill Him.... Then came the day of Unleavened Bread, when the Passover must be killed. And He sent Peter and John, saying, Go and prepare us the Passover, that we may eat.... And they made ready the Passover. And when the hour was come, He sat down, and the twelve Apostles with Him, And He said unto them, With desire I have desired to eat this Passover with you before I suffer; for I say unto you, I will not any more eat thereof, until it be fulfilled in the kingdom of God. [Blessed are they which are called unto the marriage supper of the Lamb. *Rev.* xix. 9.].... And He took bread, and gave thanks, and break it, and gave unto them, saying, This is my body which is given for you: this do in remembrance of me. Likewise also the cup after supper, saying, This cup is the new testament in my blood, which is shed for you. *Luke* xxii. 1–20.

Thus the Priest after the order of Melchisedec instituted the new Feast of the Passover.

That same night, Thursday, Jesus was seized and led to the High Priest's house. And as soon as it was day, on Friday, they led Him into their Council. (*Luke* xxii. 47.–66.) And that same day they crucified Him. (xxiii. 33.) He lay in the tomb on the Sabbath; And:—

Upon the first day of the week, [Sunday, or the Lord's Day—*not* the Sabbath] very early in the morning, [the women] came unto the sepulchre, bringing spices.... And they found the stone rolled away from the sepulchre. And they entered in, and found not the body of the Lord Jesus.... And, behold, two men stood by them in shining garments.... and said....He is not here, but is risen: remember how He spake unto you when He was yet in Galilee, saying, The Son of man must be delivered into the hands of sinful men, and be crucified, and the third day rise again. *Luke* xxiv. 1–7.

The time of keeping the Passover was fixed on the fourteenth day of the moon of March. The Feast of Easter, which is the Christian Passover, is of great antiquity. It is mentioned in Acts:— When Herod had apprehended Peter, "he put him in prison.... intending after EASTER to bring him forth to the people." *Acts* xii. 1–4. The proper day on which it is to be observed:—

Is always the first Sunday after the full moon which happens upon, or next after, the 21st day of March; and if the full moon happen upon a Sunday, Easter Day is the Sunday after. *Table of feasts.*

As we keep Sunday, the Lord's Day, instead of Saturday, the Jewish Sabbath, so we keep Easter on the Lord's Day, instead of on Friday, the precise day of the Passover, because it is not only our Lord's death, but His rising again, that shall raise us up from death.

The time is past for feasting in the Church on the fat of lambs, and "Christ our Passover is sacrificed for us." 1 *Cor.* v. 7. He has fulfilled the type of the Passover; and the Church at Easter, as near the anniversary of the Passover as she can fix it, keeps the feast spiritually, "not with the old leaven, neither with the leaven of malice and wickedness; but with the unleavened bread of sincerity and truth." 1 *Cor.* v. 7, 8.

In so doing the Church continues to obey the express appointment of the Lord to keep the Feast *as an ordinance for ever*, at the very time set by Him. It would seem that He chose this Feast as the time of His death on the Cross, that He might substitute for the type the commemorative spiritual feast represented by the bread and wine.

THE FEAST OF PENTECOST — WHITSUNTIDE.

The Feast of Weeks was kept seven weeks after the Passover:—

Seven weeks shalt thou number unto thee: begin to number the seven weeks from such time as thou beginnest to put the sickle to the corn. And thou shalt keep the Feast of Weeks unto the Lord thy God with a tribute of a freewill offering of thine hand, which thou shalt give unto the Lord thy God according as the Lord thy God hath blessed thee. *Deut.* xvi. 9, 10.

It is also called the "Feast of Harvest, the first fruits of thy labours, which thou hast sown in the field." *Ex.* xxiii. 16. The barley harvest which began at the Passover, ended at this time, seven weeks, or fifty days, after. (*Levit.* xxiii. 15, 16.) Hence it was also called, the Feast of Pentecost, Pentecost meaning *fiftieth*.

The Children of Israel journeyed forty six days after the Passover which they kept in Egypt, before they came to Mount Sinai. Moses came down from the Mount four days after, that is, the *fiftieth* day after the Passover, and delivered to them the *firstfruits* of the Law. Thus the offering of the firstfruits of the harvest at the Feast of Pentecost was a continual memorial of God's double mercy in giving His people bread to eat, and the bread of life in His Law.

Joel had prophesied:—

I will *pour out my* SPIRIT *upon all flesh*; and your sons and your daughters shall prophesy. *Joel* ii. 28.

And Jesus had said to His disciples:—

Behold, I send the promise of my Father upon you: but tarry ye in the City of Jerusalem, until ye be endued with power from on high. *Luke* xxiv. 49.

When the day of Pentecost was fully come, they were all with one accord in one place. And suddenly there came a sound from heaven as of a rushing mighty wind, and it filled all the house where they were sitting. And there appeared unto them cloven tongues like as of fire, and it sat upon each of them. And they were all *filled with the* HOLY GHOST, and began to *speak with other tongues* as the Spirit gave them utterance.... But this is that which was spoken by the prophet Joel. *Acts* ii. 1-4, 16.

St. Paul was careful to keep this feast at Jerusalem:—

For Paul had determined to sail by Ephesus, because he would not spend the time in Asia: for he hasted, if it were possible for him, to be at Jerusalem the day of Pentecost. *Acts* xx. 16.

When they desired him to tarry longer time with them, he consented not; But bade them farewell, saying, I must by all means keep this feast that cometh in Jerusalem: but I will return again unto you, if God will. And he sailed from Ephesus. *Acts* xviii. 20, 21.

The Church keeps this feast under the name of Whitsuntide, fifty days after Easter, in commemoration both of the firstfruits of the Law from Mount Sinai, and of the firstfruits of the Holy Spirit, the promised Comforter. It is evidently not accidental, nor is it the contrivance of man, that this type of the Pentecost was so exactly fulfilled at that time; for it was the Lord Himself who bade His disciples wait in Jerusalem–the appointed place for the Feast–for the promised Comforter; and it was He who sent the Comforter at the very time when the day of Pentecost was fully come. Thus did He substitute another spiritual feast for one which was a type of it. The Church in keeping the Feast of Whitsuntide, conforms no less strictly to the arrangement made by the Lord, than did the Church of Israel in keeping the Feast of Weeks, or Pentecost, commanded by Him as *a statute for ever*.

THE FEAST OF TABERNACLES — CHRISTMAS.

The Feast of Tabernacles was also called, The Feast of Ingathering. *Exodus* xxiii. 16.

In the fifteenth day of the seventh month, when ye have gathered in the fruit of the land, ye shall keep a feast unto the Lord seven days.... And ye shall take you on the first day the boughs of goodly trees, branches of palm trees, and the boughs of thick trees, and willows of the brook; and ye shall rejoice before the Lord your God seven days.... It shall be *a statute for ever* in your generations.... Ye shall dwell in booths seven days; all that are Israelites born shall dwell in booths: That your generations may know that I made the Children of Israel to dwell in booths, when I brought them out of the land of Egypt: I am the Lord your God. *Levit.* xxiii. 39–43.

Zechariah says of the importance of this feast:—

This shall be the punishment of Egypt, and the punishment of all nations that come not up to keep the Feast of Tabernacles.... Even upon them shall be no rain. *Zech.* xiv. 16–19.

When Nehemiah and Ezra were trying to bring the Children of Israel back to their ancient observance of the Law:—

They found written in the Law which the Lord commanded by Moses, that the Children of Israel should dwell in booths in the feast of the seventh month: And that they should publish and proclaim in all their cities, and in Jerusalem, saying, Go forth unto the mount, and fetch olive branches, and pine branches, and myrtle branches, and palm branches, and branches of thick trees, to make booths, as it is written. So the people went forth, and brought them, and made themselves booths, every one upon the roof of his house, and in their courts, and in the courts of the house of God, and in the street of the water gate, and in the street of the gate of Ephraim. And all the congregation of them that were come again out of the captivity made booths, and sat under the booths: for since the days of Jeshua the son of Nun unto that day had not the Children of Israel done so. And there was very great gladness. *Neh.* viii. 14–17.

Calmet says in reference to the manner in which the Israelites kept the Feast of Tabernacles:—

The first day of the feast they cut down branches

of the handsomest trees with their fruit; branches of palm trees, or such as were fullest of leaves, and boughs of the willow trees that grew by the water courses. The neatest of these branches they carried in ceremony to the synagogue, where they performed what they called *Lulab, i. e.* holding in their right hand a branch of a palm tree, three branches of myrtle, and two of willow, tied together; and having in their left hand a branch of citron with its fruit; they brought them together, waving them toward the four quarters of the world, and singing certain songs. These branches were also called Hosanna, because they cried Hosanna! not unlike what the Jews did at our Saviour's entry into Jerusalem. (*John* xii. 12-16.)

Isaiah says:—

Arise, shine; for thy light is come, and the glory of the Lord is risen upon thee. For, behold, the darkness shall cover the earth, and gross darkness the people: but the Lord shall arise upon thee, and His glory shall be seen upon thee. And the Gentiles shall come to thy light, and kings to the brightness of thy rising .... The glory of Lebanon shall come unto thee, the fir tree, the pine tree, and the box together, to beautify the place of my sanctuary. *Is.* lx. 1-3, 13.

Compare this with the following passages from the First Lesson appointed to be read on Christmas Day:—

The people that walked in darkness have seen a great light: they that dwell in the land of the shadow of death, upon them hath the light shined. Thou hast multiplied the nation, and not increased the joy: they joy before thee according to the joy *in harvest,* [Feast of Ingathering] and as men rejoice when they divide the spoil.... For unto us a *Child is born,* unto us a

Son is given: and the government shall be upon His shoulder: and His name shall be called Wonderful, Counsellor, The mighty God, The everlasting Father, The Prince of Peace. *Isaiah* ix. 2–6.

Dr. Jennings says as to the Feast of Tabernacles:

The learned Jos. Mede's opinion seems to be the most probable, as well as the most ingenious, namely, that this feast was fixed at this time of year when Christ was to be born, and the dwelling in tabernacles was intended as a type of His incarnation, as St. John intimates:—And the Word was made flesh, and *dwelt* among us. *John* i. 14.

The word *dwelt* in the original, says Dr. Whitby, properly signifies *tabernacled* among us: and has an affinity to the Hebrew word used to express God's dwelling by the Shekinah, or glorious symbol of His presence. This Shekinah was wanting in the second temple, and the defect was now repaired by the habitation of the divine nature in the temple of Christ's body.

The Shekinah, or glorious Light alluded to by Isaiah, was seen by Israel on many occasions:—

Then a cloud covered the tent of the congregation, and the glory of the Lord filled the Tabernacle. *Exodus* xl. 34.

It seems plain that the Jews were to keep this feast to remind them not only that they dwelt in tabernacles while travelling from Egypt, the land of bondage, to their land of promise; but also of that glorious presence of God which was at that same time visible in His tabernacle which they bore along with them. But the tabernacle and the temple typefied the Lord's Body—first His human body in which He was for a time tabernacled, (Destroy this temple, and in three days I will raise it up.... But He spake of the temple of His body. *John* ii. 19, 21.); and then His body the Church. (The head over all things to the Church, which is His body. *Eph.* i. 22, 23.)

Isaiah says:—

The Lord will create upon every dwelling place of Mount Zion, and upon her assemblies, a cloud and smoke by day, and the shining of a flaming fire by night: for upon all the glory shall be a defence. And there shall be a *tabernacle* for a shadow in the day time from the heat, and for a place of refuge, and for a covert from the storm and from rain. *Is.* iv. 5, 6.

Ezekiel explains this:—

My *tabernacle* also shall be with them: yea, I will be their God, and they shall be my people. *Ezek.* xxx. 27.

As St. John also says:—

I heard a great voice out of heaven saying, Behold the *tabernacle* of God is with men, and He will dwell with them. *Rev.* xxi. 3.

Our Lord gave sanction to the custom of keeping this feast, and appropriated it to Himself, when;—

In the last day, that great day of the feast [of tabernacles, v. 2.] Jesus stood and cried, saying, If any man thirst, let him come unto me, and drink. He that believeth on me, as the Scripture hath said, out of his belly shall flow rivers of living water. But this spake He of the Spirit, which they that believe on Him should receive: for the Holy Ghost was not yet given; because that Jesus was not yet glorified. *John* vii. 2, 37–39.

Isaiah makes a reference to the *willows* in unmistakable connection with the promised blessing to Israel through Christ the Redeemer:—

Fear not, O Jacob, my servant; and thou Jesurun whom I have chosen. For I will pour water upon him that is thirsty, and floods upon the dry ground: I will pour my Spirit upon thy seed, and my blessing upon thine offspring: And they shall spring up as among the grass, as *willows by the water courses*.... Thus saith the Lord the King of Israel, and his Redeemer the Lord of hosts; I am the first, and I am the last; and beside me there is no God. *Is.* xliv. 2-6.—See *John* iv. 14.—*Rev.* i. 10-18.—xxii. 13, 17.

[The above quotation from Isaiah formed a part of the Old Testament Lesson for the First Sunday after the Epiphany, or the Manifestation of Christ to the Gentiles; but the first part (vs. 2-4) has unfortunately been omitted in the new Lectionary.]

It is fitting that the Christian Church should perpetuate the Jews' Feast of Tabernacles by keeping Christmas Day, the Nativity of our Lord and Saviour Jesus Christ; and by beautifying the place of His Sanctuary with goodly boughs of the fir tree, the pine tree, and the box. She thus celebrates yearly the ingathering of the harvest of His redeemed people, for whom He was tabernacled in the flesh; while she fulfils the command to keep the statute *for ever*.

In the Collect for Christmas Day allusion is made to His tabernacling in the flesh; and to the Holy Spirit which they that believe on Him should receive:—

ALMIGHTY God, who hast given us thy only begotten Son to take our nature upon Him, and as at this time to be born of a pure Virgin; grant that we, being regenerate and made thy children by adoption and grace, may daily be renewed by thy Holy Spirit, through the same our Lord Jesus Christ, who liveth and reigneth with thee and the same Spirit, ever one God, world without end. *Amen.*

CHAPTER VII.

THE TRUMPET.

———:o:———

At Morning Prayer, on the sixteenth day of the month, the Church uses Psalm lxxxi. The following is the Psalter version of the first four verses:—

Sing we merrily unto God our strength; make a cheerful noise unto the God of Jacob.

Take the psalm, bring hither the tabret, the merry harp with the lute.

Blow up the *trumpet* in the *new moon,* even in the time appointed, and upon our solemn feast day.

For this was made a statute for Israel, and a law of the God of Jacob.

The Jews kept the Feast of the New moon at the beginning of each month: So it is the custom of the Church to administer the Holy Communion on the first Sunday of each month. This is the command for keeping the Feast of Trumpets:—

In the seventh month, on the first day of the month ye shall have an holy convocation; ye shall do no servile work: it is a day of blowing the trumpets unto you. *Numbers* xxix. 1.

Bishop Horne says:—

This seventh month was specially marked, and its

new moon was a solemn feast day which had a particular regard paid to it, because according to the old calculation, before Israel came out of Egypt, it was the first new moon in the year, which began this day, the first of the (afterwards) seventh month. The tenth of the same month was the great Day of Atonement; and on the fifteenth was celebrated the Feast of the Tabernacles. (*Numbers* xxix. 7-12.)

It is not strange that we should find in the use of the trumpet, as God commanded Moses, a part of that emblematic ceremonial which prefigured to Israel things yet for to come. Their prophet Isaiah told them:—

It shall come to pass in that day, that the *Great Trumpet* shall be blown, and they shall come which were ready to perish in the land of Assyria, and the outcasts in the land of Egypt, and shall worship the Lord in the holy mount at Jerusalem. *Is.* xxvii. 13.

The silver trumpets were made according to an express command, and were used to *assemble the Congregation*; and this was to be a perpetual ordinance:—

The Lord spake unto Moses, saying, Make thee two trumpets of silver; of a whole piece shalt thou make them: that thou mayest use them for the calling of the Assembly, and for the journeying of the camps. And when they shall blow with them, all the assembly shall assemble themselves to thee at the door of the tabernacle of the Congregation.... And the sons of Aaron, the priests, shall blow with the trumpets; and they shall be to you for an ordinance for ever throughout your generations. *Num.* x. 1-3, 8.

These were the occasions prescribed for using the silver trumpets:—

If ye go to war in your land against the enemy that oppresseth you, then ye shall blow an alarm with the trumpets; and ye shall *be numbered* before the Lord your God, and ye shall be saved from your enemies. Also in the day of your gladness, and in your solemn days, and in the beginnings of your months, ye shall blow with the trumpets over your burnt offerings, and over the sacrifices of your peace offerings; that they may be to you for a memorial before your God. *Numbers* x. 9, 10.

When the law was given on Mount Sinai:—

It came to pass on the third day in the morning, that there were thunders and lightnings, and a thick cloud upon the Mount, and the voice of the *trumpet* exceeding loud; so that all the people that was in the camp trembled. *Exodus* xix. 16.

All the people saw the thunderings, and the lightnings, and the noise of the trumpet, and the mountain smoking. *Exodus* xx. 18.

St. Paul tells us that the Law:—

Was ordained by *angels* in the hand of a mediator. *Galatians* iii. 19.—And St. Stephen says of Moses:—

This is he, that was in the church in the wilderness with the Angel which spake to him in the Mount Sina. and with our fathers: who received the lively oracles to give unto us. *Acts* vii. 38.

And he denounces the Jews:—

Who have received the Law by the *disposition of angels*, and have not kept it. *Acts* vii. 51–53.

It thus seems that the trumpet sounds were signs of the presence of Him:—

Who maketh His angels spirits; His ministers a flaming fire. *Psalm* civ. 4.—Are they not all ministering spirits, sent forth to minister for them who shall be heirs of salvation? *Hebrews* i. 14.

St. Paul tells us:—

We shall not all sleep, but we shall all be changed, in a moment, in the twinkling of an eye, at the last trump: for the TRUMPET shall sound, and the dead shall be raised incorruptible, and we shall be changed. 1 *Corinthians* xv. 51, 52.

David says:—

God is gone up with a shout, the Lord with the sound of a *trumpet*. *Psalm* xlvii. 5.

As He ascended after His resurrection, so:—

The Lord Himself shall descend from heaven with a shout, with the voice of the Archangel, and with the *trump* of God: and the dead in Christ shall rise. 1 *Thess.* iv. 16.

As the Lord Himself saith:—

They shall see the Son of man coming in the clouds of heaven with power and great glory. And He shall send His *angels* with a great sound of a *trumpet*, and they shall gather together His elect from the four winds, from one end of heaven to the other. [they shall *be numbered* before the Lord.] *Matt.* xxiv. 30, 31.

The Church recognizes the ministration of the angels, mysterious and unseen though it be, remembering what David says:—

He shall give His angels charge over thee, to keep thee in all thy ways. They shall bear thee up in their hands, lest thou dash thy foot against a stone. *Ps.* xci. 11, 12.

A day—September 29th—called "The Feast of St. Michael and all Angels," is set apart to meditate upon this subject. This is one of the means by which we can prepare for that dread moment when we shall come to realize St. John's vision:—

I was in the Spirit on the Lord's day, and heard behind me a great voice, as of a TRUMPET, Saying, I am ALPHA and OMEGA, the FIRST and the LAST. *Revelation* i. 10, 11.

By the use of the Gospel appointed for that day the Church would correct a wrong idea, that children, and saintly persons become *angels* after death. The Collect shows the proper interpretation of the passage:—"In heaven their angels do always behold the face of my Father which is in heaven;" while it also instructs us that we are not to address our prayers to angels, or spirits, but to their God, and our God, for:—

There is one Mediator between God and men, the man Christ Jesus. 1 *Timothy* ii. 5.

O EVERLASTING God, who hast ordained and constituted the services of Angels and men in a wonderful order; mercifully grant, that as thy holy Angels always do thee service in heaven; so, by thy appointment, they may succour and defend us on earth, through Jesus Christ our Lord. *Amen.*

CHAPTER VIII.

THE SEVEN CANDLESTICKS.

———:o:———

When the Lord commanded Moses to make the Tabernacle, and all the implements for its service, He said, "See that thou make all things according to the pattern shewed to thee in the Mount." *Ex.* xxv. 40.—*Heb.* viii. 5. And the priests who offered gifts according to the law, served "unto the example and *shadow* of heavenly things." *Heb.* viii. 5.—In the Tabernacle was a candlestick of gold, with six branches—*seven* in all—and the lamps thereof gave their light. *Ex.* xxv. 31-37. Of what may this candlestick have been the shadow? In the Scriptures seven is a sacred, mystic number. The Jews supposed it to represent God. The seventh day of the week, and the seventh years, were devoted to the Lord. Seven is also applied in a curious manner to the Holy Spirit of God; and when mention occurs of "The Seven Spirits" in connection with the Father and the Son, it is undoubtedly a grouping of the persons of the Holy Trinity. Thus, St. John says:—

John to the *seven* churches which are in Asia: Grace be unto you, and peace, from Him which is, and which was, and which is to come; and from the *Seven Spirits* which are before His throne; And from Jesus Christ who is the faithful witness, and the first begotten of the dead, and the Prince of the kings of the earth. *Revelation* i. 4, 5.

St. John in his Apocalyptic vision often speaks of the *Seven Spirits* of God which are before His throne: And he applies the type of the seven candlesticks not only to the seven Spirits, but to the seven Churches. From this it may be inferred that the seven Spirits represent the *one* Holy Spirit; and the seven Churches, the *one* Holy Church of which He is the light. Zechariah saw a candlestick all of gold, with a bowl upon the top of it and his *seven lamps* thereon. And the Angel told him that the signification was:—

This is the word of the Lord unto Zerubbabel, saying, Not by might, nor by power, but by my *Spirit*, saith the Lord of hosts. *Zech.* iv. 1–6.

St. John seems to explain this in his vision:—

There were *seven lamps* of fire burning before the throne, which are the *Seven Spirits* of God. *Rev.* iv. 5.

When St. John saw seven candlesticks, and in the midst of them One like unto the Son of man, having in His right hand seven stars, He told him:

The seven stars which thou sawest in my right hand, are the angels [bishops] of the seven Churches: and the seven candlesticks which thou sawest are the seven Churches. *Rev.* i. 8–20.

The Lord Jesus Christ, both as the Lamb, and as the Stone, is represented as having the seven Spirits of God.

First, As the Lamb:—

The Root of David hath prevailed to open the book, and to loose the *seven* seals thereof. And I beheld, and, lo, in the midst of the throne and of the four beasts, and in the midst of the elders, stood a Lamb, as it had been slain, having seven horns, and seven eyes, which are the seven Spirits of God sent forth into all the earth. *Rev.* v. 5, 6.

And the thousands around the throne said:—

Worthy is the Lamb that was slain to receive power, and riches, and wisdom, and strength, and honour, and glory, and blessing;—Seven attributes. *Rev.* v. 12.

Second, As the Stone:—

Behold, I will bring forth my servant The Branch. For, behold, the Stone that I have laid before Joshua; upon one Stone shall be seven eyes: behold, I will engrave the graving thereof, saith the Lord of hosts. *Zechariah* iii. 8, 9.

This graving by the Lord Himself upon the Stone, contained the law and the ten commandments of the Church of Israel and of the Church of Christ; one link by which the two Churches are connected. At Mount Sinai:—

The Lord said unto Moses, Come up to me into the Mount, and be there: and I will give thee tables of *stone*, and a law, and commandments which I have written; that thou mayest teach them. *Ex.* xxiv. 12.

And Moses turned, and went down from the Mount, and the two tables of the testimony were in his hand. .... And the tables were the work of God, and the writing was the writing of God, graven upon the tables. *Exodus* xxxii. 15, 16.

David says:—

The *Stone* which the builders refused is become the head stone of the corner. *Psalm* cxviii. 22.

And St. Paul:—

Through Him we both have access by one Spirit unto the Father.... And are built upon the foundation of the Apostles and Prophets, Jesus Christ Himself being the chief corner stone; In whom all the building fitly framed together groweth unto an holy temple in the Lord: In whom ye also are builded together for an habitation of God through the Spirit. *Eph.* ii. 18-22.—Again, St. Peter says:—

Ye also, as lively stones, are built up a spiritual house, an holy priesthood, to offer up spiritual sacrifices, acceptable to God by Jesus Christ. Wherefore also it is contained in the Scripture, Behold, I lay in Sion a *Chief Corner Stone*, elect, precious: and he that believeth on Him shall not be confounded. Unto you therefore which believe He is precious: but unto them which be disobedient, the Stone which the builders disallowed, the same is made the head of the corner. 1 *Peter* ii. 5-7.—*Isaiah* xxviii. 16.

So, He who hath the Seven Spirits—the one perfect Spirit—of God, is the Chief Corner Stone of the one perfect Church. And as the tabernacle and the temple were composed of several parts fitly framed together, forming one building for the service of God, so the members of the Church, as lively stones each having his place and office, are by keeping His law and commandments, built up a spiritual house for the acceptable worship of God. *Eph.* ii. 19-22.—iv. 15, 16.

St. Paul says: "There is one Spirit, but diversities of gifts." *Rom.* xii. 6.–1 *Cor.* xii. 4.–*Heb.* ii. 4. And the mystical number *seven* is used in describing the gifts, in several places, like these which follow:—

The words of the Lord [wisdom] are pure words: as silver tried in a furnace of earth, purified *seven* times. *Psalm* xii. 6.

Wisdom hath builded her house, she hath hewn out her *seven* pillars. *Prov.* ix. 1. Seven pillars—the seven Spirits of God, which is perfect wisdom.

The diversity of gifts of the Spirit is thus described by St. Paul:—

The manifestation of the Spirit is given to every man to profit withal. For to one is given by the Spirit the *Word of wisdom*; to another the *Word of knowledge* by the same Spirit; to another *faith* by the same Spirit;...... to another *prophecy*; [or the gift of teaching] to another *discerning of spirits*; to another *divers kinds of tongues*; to another the *interpretation of tongues*. 1 *Cor.* xii. 7-10.

The Prophet Isaiah says:—

There shall come forth a Rod out of the stem of Jesse, and a Branch [the same Branch spoken of by

Zechariah as having the seven eyes, which are the seven Spirits of God] shall grow out of his roots: And the Spirit of the Lord shall rest upon Him, [as the Lord of hosts engraved the seven eyes upon the stone] the spirit of *wisdom* and *understanding*, the spirit of *counsel* and *might*, the spirit of *knowledge* and of the *fear of the Lord*.... With *righteousness* shall He judge the poor, and reprove with equity for the meek of the earth. *Isaiah* xi. 1–4.

Here are *seven* diverse gifts of the Spirit. And as these gifts are communicated to each member of the Church, through its ordinances and services, "according as God hath dealt to every man the measure of faith," (*Rom.* xii. 3.) it may be inferred that the seven candlesticks which gave light in the Tabernacle, were the *shadow* of the Spirit which lights up the Church, and is reflected from its worthy members according as they show forth the fruits of the Spirit.

The true and perfect Church shall only be seen in all its glory in Heaven. The candlestick with its seven lamps gave light to the Tabernacle: but the Church thus typefied :–

Hath no need of candle, neither light of the sun, neither of the moon, to shine in it; for the glory of God doth lighten it, and the Lamb is the light thereof. *Revelation* xxi. 23.—xxii. 5.

How remarkably is this prophesied by Isaiah with the use of the mystical number:–

Moreover the light of the moon shall be as the light of the sun, and the light of the sun shall be *sevenfold*, as the light of *seven* days, in the day that the Lord bindeth up the breach of His people, and healeth the stroke of their wound. *Isaiah* xxx. 26.

The solemn ritual of the Church of Israel, with its glorious temple, has passed away. Its types are fulfilled. Its place is supplied in the Church of the new covenant, gathered from Jews and Gentiles, by a *spiritual* worship which has superseded the worship through types and shadows. This Church has the reality of gifts and sacrifices which could only be foreshadowed in the Church of Israel; for the Messiah has come to take away "sacrifice and offering and burnt offerings and offering for sin" which were offered by the Law, through the offering of His body once for all. (*Heb.* x. 8-10.) And since the Lord's ascension into heaven, the sevenfold Spirit the Comforter has come. *Acts* ii.

By its rite of Confirmation, in which the prayer taken from Isaiah is used in confirming its lively members in their fit places in the body, the Church strikingly recalls the type of the Tabernacle and its seven candlesticks. A number of her children made members of her body in baptism, assemble before one of her Angels—the Bishop—ready to confess her faith before the congregation, and anxious to exercise with fidelity the gifts which God hath dealt to them. The Bishop having heard their renewal of their baptismal vows, before confirming them with *laying on of his hands*, prays in words which remind them of the promises of God in their behalf. He then invokes upon them the sevenfold Spirit of God:—

ALMIGHTY and everliving God, who hast vouchsafed to regenerate these thy Servants by water and the Holy Ghost, and hast given unto them forgiveness of all their sins; strengthen them, we beseech thee, O Lord, with the Holy Ghost, the Comforter;

and daily increase in them thy manifold gifts of grace; the spirit of *wisdom* and *understanding*, the spirit of *counsel* and *ghostly strength*, the spirit of *knowledge* and true *godliness*; and fill them, O Lord, with the spirit of thy *holy fear*, now and for ever. *Amen.*

CHAPTER IX.

THE EPIPHANY STAR.

———:0:———

Where is He that is born King of the Jews? for we have seen His STAR in the East, and are come to worship Him. *Matt.* ii. 2.

The wise men in the East saw the Star:—

And, lo, the Star, which they saw in the East, went before them, till it came and stood over where the young child was. When they saw the Star, they rejoiced with exceeding great joy. *Matt.* ii. 9, 10.

Was this one of the stars of heaven, leaving its place, and miraculously serving this special purpose? Or what was it? Balaam took up his parable and said:—

There shall come a Star out of Jacob, and a Sceptre shall rise out of Israel. *Num.* xxiv. 17.

And St. Luke says that when the Angel of the Lord appeared to the shepherds to reveal to them the birth of Christ, "The *Glory of the Lord* shone round about them." *Luke* ii. 9.

Perhaps, then, it was the glorious light of the Lord, the *Shekinah*, which assumed the form of a brilliant star, that by the literal fulfilment of prophesy, it might identify Him as the realization of that "Light to lighten the Gentiles, and the *glory* of thy people Israel," which the prophets foretold, (*Is.* ix. 2.—xlii. 6.—xlix. 6.) and which holy Simeon recognized. (*Luke* ii. 25-32.) It might also point the rebuke which St. Stephen, quoting the prophet Amos, gave the Jews:-

Then God turned, and gave them up to worship the host of heaven; as it is written in the book of the prophets, O ye house of Israel, have ye offered to me slain beasts and sacrifices by the space of forty years in the wilderness? Yea, ye took up the tabernacle of Moloch, and the *star* of your god Remphan, figures which ye made to worship them: and I will carry you away beyond Babylon. *Acts* vii. 42, 43.—*Amos* v. 25.

Isaiah, prophesying that the "Redeemer shall come to Zion," (*Is.* lix. 20.) exclaims:-

Arise, shine; for thy *Light* is come, and the *Glory of the Lord* is risen upon thee. For, behold, the darkness shall cover the earth, and gross darkness the people: but the Lord shall arise upon thee, and His glory shall be seen upon thee. And the Gentiles shall come to thy Light, and kings to the brightness of thy rising. *Isaiah* lx. 1-3.

The Shekinah, or glorious appearance, by which the Lord made known His presence to men, was often in the form of a cloud, or of fire. It was tempered so that men in beholding it would not be destroyed by its brightness; as the Glory of the Godhead was veiled in Christ under the form of humanity.

When Moses said to the Lord, "I beseech thee show me thy glory," the Lord said:-

Thou canst not see my face: for there shall no man see me, and live...... I will put thee in a clift of the

Rock, and will cover thee with my hand while I pass by.... I will make all my goodness pass before thee. *Exodus* xxxiii. 18–23.

The Angel of the Lord appeared unto Moses in a *flame of fire* out of the midst of a bush; and he looked and, behold, the bush burned with fire, and the bush was not consumed. *Exodus* iii. 2.

When the Lord would make a covenant with Abraham, whereby he should know that the land of Canaan should be his inheritance:—
He entered into a formal ritual covenant with him after the manner of men. It was the most solemn of all forms of ratifying a treaty or covenant among divers ancient nations, and among the rest of Chaldeans (as may be seen from *Jer.* xxxiv. 18.), to divide the carcass of a victim, as butchers divide a sheep, into two equal parts lengthwise. These were placed opposite to each other, and the covenanting parties entering at the opposite extremities of the passage thus formed, met in the middle and there took the oath. Accordingly Abraham was directed thus to divide and lay out a heifer, a she-goat, a ram, a turtle dove, and a young pigeon. These he watched to protect them from birds of prey, and to wait the expected manifestation. As the sun was going down, the great and darksome horror, and the partial unconsciousness–unconsciousness of his clayey burden–that fell upon him, disclosed to Abraham that God was sensibly near. He heard a voice declaring to him the destiny of his sons for four generations, after which they should come triumphant from bondage to take possession of that land. The voice ceased–the darkness deepened–and, lo, a *flaming fire* in the midst of what seemed like the smoke of a furnace, passed between the pieces. This

was the well known symbol of the Divine presence; and thus was the covenant ratified by the most solemn sanction known in ancient times among men. *Kitto.*

When Israel fled from Egypt:—

The Lord went before them by day in a *pillar of a cloud,* to lead them the way; and by night in a *pillar of fire,* to give them light. *Ex.* xiii. 21.

And when the Egyptians pursued them:—

The Angel of God which went before the camp of Israel, removed, and went behind them: and the pillar of the cloud went from before their face, and stood behind them: And it came between the camp of the Egyptians and the camp of Israel; and it was a cloud and darkness to them, but it gave light by night to these; so that the one came not near the other all the night.... The Lord looked unto the host of the Egyptians through the pillar of fire and of the cloud, and troubled the host of the Egyptians. *Ex.* xiv. 19–24.

Perhaps it was in reference to this that Isaiah promised that if the house of Jacob would keep the fast which the Lord hath chosen:—

Then shall thy light break forth as the morning, and thine health shall spring forth speedily: and thy righteousness shall go before thee; and the *glory of the Lord* shall be thy *rere-ward.* *Is.* lviii 6–8.

At the giving of the Law to Israel:—

Mount Sinai was altogether on a smoke, because the Lord descended upon it in fire. *Ex.* xix. 18.

When the Lord punished Korah:—

It came to pass when the congregation was gathered against Moses and against Aaron, that they looked toward the tabernacle of the congregation: and, behold, the cloud covered it and the *glory of the Lord* appeared. *Numbers* xvi. 42.

After Moses had set up the Tabernacle according to God's command:—

Then a *cloud* covered the tent of the congregation, and the *glory of the Lord* filled the Tabernacle. And Moses was not able to enter into the tent of the congregation, because the cloud abode thereon, and the glory of the Lord filled the Tabernacle. *Ex.* xl. 34.

When the Lord gave commandment concerning the details and service of the Tabernacle, He said:—

There I will meet with the children of Israel, and the Tabernacle shall be sanctified by my glory. *Ex.* xxix. 43.—As Moses entered into the Tabernacle, the *cloudy pillar* descended, and stood at the door of the Tabernacle, and the Lord talked with Moses. *Ex.* xxxiii.

The Lord also appeared in the cloud upon the mercy seat in the Tabernacle. (*Levit.* xvi. 2.) So when the Temple was consecrated:—

When Solomon had made an end of praying, the fire came down from heaven, and consumed the burnt offering and the sacrifices; and the *glory of the Lord* filled the house. And the priests could not enter into the house of the Lord, because the glory of the Lord had filled the Lord's house. 2 *Chron.* vii. 1, 2.

Solomon's temple was destroyed, and the Jews were carried into captivity. In the time of Cyrus king of Persia:—

Began Zerubbabel, and Jeshua, and the remnant of their brethren the priests and the Levites, and all that were come out of the captivity unto Jerusalem; and appointed the Levites, from twenty years old and upward, to set forward the work of the house of the Lord...... But many of the priests and Levites and chief of the fathers, who were ancient men, that had seen the first house, when the foundation of this house was laid before their eyes, wept with a loud voice. *Ezra* iii. 8, 12.

Of this new temple the prophet Haggai says:—

Who is left among you that saw this house in her first glory? and how do ye see it now? is it not in your eyes in comparison of it as nothing?—And then he predicts of it:—

I will shake all nations, and the DESIRE of all nations shall come: and I will fill this house with glory, saith the Lord of hosts.... The glory of this latter house shall be greater than of the former, saith the Lord of hosts: and in this place will I give *peace*.-[My covenant of peace. *See chapter* ii. *Covenant of the Rainbow.*] *Haggai* ii. 3, 7, 9.

When He, the Desire of all nations, the Prince of Peace, thus clearly predicted by Haggai, was transfigured on the mountain:—

His face did shine as the sun, and His raiment was white as the light.... and a *bright cloud* overshadowed them: and behold a voice out of the cloud, which said, This is my beloved Son, in whom I am well pleased. *Matt.* xvii. 2, 5.

As St. Paul journeyed:—

He came near Damascus: and suddenly there shined round about him a *light from heaven*: And he fell to the earth, and heard a voice saying unto him, Saul, Saul, why persecutest thou me? And he said, Who art thou, Lord? And the Lord said, I am Jesus, whom thou persecutest. *Acts* ix. 3-5.

The Shekinah illumined the first temple, which was destroyed because of the wickedness of the Jews. The second temple, built under Zerubbabel was far inferior to the former. The Ark, the Mercy-seat, the Urim and Thummim, were not restored, and the Shekinah did not appear in it. The obscuring of the operation of the Holy Spirit in the Church was thus typified. The word Shekinah signifies, Divine presence, tabernacling. The Jews understand by it the presence of the Holy Spirit. In the Son of man the glorious Shekinah again illumined the Church; but through the wickedness of the Jews who crucified Him, it was again obscured. It shall burst forth in all its brightness when that "*Bright and morning Star*" (*Rev.* xxii. 16.) shall guide and lead us on to the tabernacle of God, "an house not made with hands, eternal in the heavens." (2 *Cor.* v. 1.)

When we shall see the glory of this latter house then will be fulfilled the type of the cloud in the Tabernacle and the Temple; for the great High Priest who was once tabernacled in the flesh, shall open to us "the temple of the tabernacle of the testimony in heaven," as described by St. John:—

The temple was filled with smoke from the glory of God, and from His power; and no man was able to enter into the temple, till the seven plagues of the seven angels were fulfilled. *Rev.* xv. 5, 8.

The obvious application of the connection with our Saviour of these manifestations of God's glory is well expressed in the Collect for The Epiphany, or the Manifestation of Christ to the Gentiles.

O GOD, who by the leading of a STAR didst manifest thy only begotten Son to the Gentiles; mercifully grant that we, who know thee now by faith, may after this life have the fruition of thy glorious Godhead, through Jesus Christ our Lord. *Amen.*

CHAPTER X.

THE TEMPLE OF THE LORD.

————:o:————

The Lord commanded Moses:—
Speak unto the children of Israel, that they bring me an offering: of every man that giveth it willingly with his heart ye shall take my offering..... And let them make me a sanctuary; that I may dwell among them. According to all that I shew thee, after the pattern of the Tabernacle, and the pattern of all the instruments thereof, even so shall ye make it. *Ex.* xxv. 2–9.—These things were to be made after the pattern which God would show, for they were to foreshadow other things to come, as St. Paul explains in his Epistle to the Hebrews, especially the ninth chapter. This symbolism pervades the Tabernacle, the Temple, the Church, and each individual member of the Church.

THE TABERNACLE.

The Tabernacle was constructed with a view to its being readily set up, and easily transported while the Israelites journeyed towards the Holy Land; symbolizing the facility with which the Church should be borne to the uttermost parts of the earth. It was made of curtains of linen covered with rams' skins, and outer coverings of badgers' skins; and of boards arranged with sockets and tenons which fitted together, and were confined by bars of wood. The boards and bars were overlaid with gold. Within the Tabernacle a place was divided off from the rest by a vail of blue, and purple, and scarlet, and fine twined linen of cunning work, with cherubims. (*Ex.* xxvi.) This was called "The Most Holy," while the rest was the "Holy place." Around the Tabernacle was the enclosure called the Court. The Ark of the Covenant in which was deposited the testimony, or tables on which the Law was written, was placed inside the vail, in the Most Holy place. The Mercy-seat was upon the Ark. (*Ex.* 16–22.)

Among the instruments for the Tabernacle, was the table upon which Shew-bread was to be set before the Lord alway, and which stood without the vail, on the North side. (*Ex.* xxv. 30—xxvi. 35.) Calmet says that the Hebrew for *shew-bread* signifies, bread of faces, or of the face. They thus called the loaves of bread which the priest of the week placed every Sabbath day on the golden table, in the Sanctum, before the Lord. These loaves were square, and had four faces: they were covered with gold: they were twelve in number, and represented the twelve tribes of Israel. Beside these loaves stood a vessel full of excellent wine, which was poured out as a libation before the Lord, when the loaves were changed at the close of the week. Here are the *bread and the wine*, as in the offering of Melchisedec to Abraham. (*Gen.* xiv. 18.)

Then there was the golden candlestick with the seven lamps. It was to be provided with pure oil by the children of Israel, "to cause the lamp to burn always." Then the Altar of burnt offering, with horns on its four corners. (*Ex.* xxvii. 1–21.) The Laver, of brass, stood between the tabernacle of the congregation and the altar. The Laver contained water for the priests :—

When they go into the Tabernacle of the congregation, they shall wash with water that they die not; or when they come near to the Altar to minister. *Ex.* xxx. 18–21.—In allusion to this David says :—

I will wash mine hands in innocency: so will I compass thine altar, O Lord. *Psalm* xxvi. 6.

According to all that the Lord commanded him so did Moses :—

Then a cloud covered the tent of the congregation, and the glory of the Lord filled the Tabernacle. *Ex.* xl. 34.—Thus the *Shekinah* appeared in the Tabernacle. There appears to be a significance in the place chosen for the Tabernacle ;—

The whole congregation of the children of Israel assembled together at *Shiloh*, and set up the Tabernacle of the congregation there. And the land was subdued before them. *Joshua* xviii. 1.

Shiloh was a city of Ephraim, about 25 miles North of Jerusalem, between Lebanon and Bethel. The Tabernacle, with the Ark of the covenant, being set up there, it became known as the holy city of the Jews, in the land "which was subdued before them." With it then was associated the idea of the presence of the Lord among His people.

About 300 years after the Tabernacle was set up at Shiloh, Israel went out to battle against the Philistines, and being defeated, they presumptuously sent and brought out the Ark, without being so commanded by the Lord. But the Philistines captured the Ark, and it was not again taken to Shiloh. (1 *Samuel* iv.)

Jeremiah shows that great desolation fell upon Shiloh after the Ark was removed from it; and the Lord by the prophet threatened Jerusalem with the same destruction if the people continued to commit presumptuous sins, while they came to stand before Him in His house. (*Jer.* vii. 8-12.)

Jacob in pronouncing his final blessing upon his sons, prophesied:-

The sceptre shall not depart from Judah, nor a lawgiver from between his feet, until SHILOH come; and *unto Him shall the gathering of the people be.* Gen. xlix. 10.—Jesus saith:-

When the Son of man shall come in His glory, and all the holy angels with Him, then shall He sit upon the throne of His glory: And *before Him shall be gathered all nations.* Matt. xxv. 31, 32.

Shiloh, or as the word signifies, The Peacemaker, or He whose right it is, came to reign in Jerusalem, "tabernacled in the flesh," and was cut off. The Lord's presence ceased from Jerusalem, its destruction soon after followed, and the Jews have never since had a ruler from their own nation; nor have they had a tabernacle.

THE TEMPLE AT JERUSALEM.

To replace the temporary tabernacle by a permanent structure, King David commanded his son Solomon, and all the princes of Israel:-

Now set your heart and your soul to seek the Lord your God; arise therefore, and build ye the sanctuary of the Lord God, to bring the Ark of the covenant of the Lord, and the holy vessels of God, into the house that is to be built to the name of the Lord. 1 *Chron.* xxii. 17-19.

Then David gave to Solomon his son the pattern of .... the place of the Mercy-seat, and the pattern of all that he had *by the Spirit*, of the courts of the house of the Lord, and of all the chambers round about. 1 *Chron.* xxviii. 11, 12.

David had prepared much gold, silver, precious stones, and other material, to build the house. (1 *Chron.* xxix. 2.) But God said unto him:—

Thou shalt not build an house for my name, because thou hast been a man of war, and hast shed blood. 1 *Chron.* xxviii. 3.

Then Solomon began to build the house of the Lord at Jerusalem in Mount Moriah, where the Lord appeared unto David his father, in the place that David had prepared in the threshing floor of Ornan the Jebusite. 2 *Chron.* iii. 1.

Jerusalem was in the possessions of the Jebusites, and fell to the lot of the tribe of Judah to which David belonged, and from which the Messiah, the Son of David, sprang.

And the house, when it was in building, was built of stone made ready before it was brought thither: so that there was neither hammer nor axe nor any tool of iron heard in the house, while it was in building. 1 *Kings* vi. 7.

Against the walls of the house *chambers* were built round about. The inside walls were covered with boards of cedar carved with open flowers, palm trees, cherubim, &c. In the temple there was a space for the Oracle, or the Most Holy place. To set there the Ark of the covenant of the Lord. And a vail hung upon chains of gold, divided the Oracle from the other part of the house. (1 *Ki.* vi.)

When the Lord Jesus yielded up the Ghost

upon the Cross, "The *vail* of the Temple was rent in twain from the top to the bottom." (*Matthew* xxvii. 51.) Then the old sacrifices were abolished, their type being fulfilled, and we now enter into the holiest "through the *vail* that is to say His flesh." *Heb.* ix, x.

For the doors of the temple posts were made of olive tree. The two doors were of fir: the leaves of the doors were folding; and cherubim, palms, and open flowers were carved on them; and they were covered with gold fitted upon the carved work. (1 *Kings* vi.)

Instead of the Laver of the Tabernacle, there was made a molten sea to hold water.

It stood upon twelve oxen, three looking toward the north, and three looking toward the west, and three looking toward the south, and three looking toward the east. 1 *Kings* vii. 23–26.

These oxen probably symbolized the patient and laborious Apostles, whose mission it was to carry the water of life to the four quarters of the earth.

And Solomon made all the vessels that pertained unto the house of the Lord: the altar of gold, and the table of gold, whereupon the shew-bread was, and the candlesticks of pure gold.... and the censers of pure gold. 1 *Kings* vii. 48–51.

Then all things were put in their place. And Solomon assembled all the chief men:-

That they might bring up the Ark of the covenant of the Lord out of the city of David, which is Zion.... And it came to pass, when the priests were come out of the holy place, that the *cloud* filled the house of the Lord, so that the priests could not stand to minister because of the cloud: for the *glory of the Lord* had filled the house of the Lord. 1 *Kings* viii. 1–11.

Thus the *Shekinah* appeared in the Temple, as it had done in the Tabernacle.

THE BRIDE, THE LAMB'S WIFE.

In the Prophets, and the Book of Revelation are many allusions to the Church in glory, which throw light on the typical meaning of the tabernacle and temple, and their instruments, while the latter in turn serve to make better understood the mysteries of the prophetic and Apocalyptic vision.

I John saw the holy city, new Jerusalem, coming down from God out of heaven, prepared as a bride adorned for her husband. And I heard a great voice out of heaven saying, Behold, the *tabernacle* of God is with men, and He will dwell with them, and they shall be His people, and God Himself shall be with them, and be their God.... And there came unto me one of the seven angels.... and talked with me, saying, Come hither, I will shew thee the *Bride*, the LAMB'S Wife. And he carried me away in the Spirit to a great and high mountain, (typified by Mount Zion) and shewed me that great city, the holy Jerusalem, descending out of heaven from God, Having the *glory of God*: and her light was like unto a *Stone most precious*, even like a jasper stone, clear as crystal. And had a wall great and high, and had twelve gates, and at the gates twelve angels, and names written thereon, which are the names of the twelve tribes of the children of Israel: On the east three gates; on the north three gates; on the south three gates; and on the west three gates. [Like the twelve oxen bearing the molten sea of the Temple.] And the wall of the city had twelve foundations, and in them the names of the twelve Apostles of the Lamb. [The household of God; built upon the foundation of the Apostles and prophets, Jesus Christ Himself being the chief corner stone. *Eph.* ii. 21, 22.].... And the building of the wall of it was of jasper: and the city was pure gold, like unto clear glass. And the foundations of the wall of the city were garnished with all manner of *precious stones*.... And the twelve gates were twelve pearls; every several gate was of *one pearl*: [one pearl of great price. *Matt.* xiii. 45.] and the street of the city was pure gold, as it were transparent glass. *Rev.* xxi. 1-21.

All this was typefied by the glory and beauty of Solomon's temple. The significance of its being of stone made ready before it was brought thither, is perhaps shown by Daniel:

Thou sawest till that a *Stone* was cut out without hands, which smote the image upon his feet that were of iron and clay, and brake them to pieces. *Dan.* ii.

Ezekiel thus speaks of the Church:—

I clothed thee also with broidered work, and shod thee with *badger's skin*, and I girded thee about with fine *linen*, and I covered thee with silk. I decked thee also with ornaments, and I put bracelets upon thy hands, and a chain on thy neck. And I put a jewel on thy forehead, and earrings in thine ears, and a beautiful crown upon thine head. Thus wast thou decked with gold and silver; and thy raiment was of fine linen, and silk, and broidered work..... and thou wast exceeding beautiful. *Ezek.* xvi. 10-13.

The Oriental women were especially particular as to the covering of their feet. The allusion to the badger skin sandals, in connection with other ornaments of the bride, represent the varieties of wealth, luxury and honour, which were bestowed by God upon the Jewish people. *W. Lowth.*

Here is St. John's vision of the Bride:—

Let us be glad and rejoice, and give honour to Him: for the marriage of the LAMB is come, and His Wife hath made herself ready. And to her was granted that she should be arrayed in fine *linen*, clean and white: for the fine linen is the *righteousness of saints*... And the armies which were in heaven followed Him upon white horses, clothed in fine linen, white and clean. *Rev.* xix. 7–14.

He that overcometh, the same shall be clothed in white raiment. *Rev.* iii. 5.

And David draws this beautiful picture of her:—

Unto the Son He saith: (*Heb.* i. 8, 9.) Thy throne, O God, is for ever and ever: the sceptre of thy kingdom is a right sceptre. Thou lovest righteousness, and hatest wickedness: therefore God, thy God, hath anointed thee with the oil of gladness above thy fellows.... Upon thy right hand did stand the *Queen* in [a vesture of, *ps. ver.*] *gold* of Ophir. Hearken, O Daughter, and incline thine ear; forget also thine own people, and thy father's house; So shall the King greatly desire thy beauty: for He is thy Lord; and worship thou Him.... The King's Daughter is all glorious within: her clothing is of wrought gold. She shall be brought unto the King in raiment of needlework. *Psalm* xlv. 6–14.

The angel stood, saying, Rise, and measure the Temple of God, and the Altar, and them that worship therein. But the *Court* which is without the Temple leave out, and measure it not; for it is given unto the

Gentiles: and the holy city shall they tread under foot forty and two months. *Rev.* xi. 1, 2.

Perhaps this passage may mean that, of those who belong in the temple, and worship at its altar, there can be no doubt; their condition can be easily understood. The Gentiles, or heathen, would for a season assault the Church, but their attacks would be confined to the outer courts, and would not reach the inner temple. Eventually they would be driven out of that part also, and have no more power to do harm. The Lord Jesus taught a similar lesson when:—

He went into the temple of God, and cast out all them that sold and bought in the Temple, and overthrew the tables of the moneychangers, and the seats of them that sold doves, And said unto them, It is written, My house shall be called the house of prayer; but ye have made it a den of thieves. *Matt.* xxi. 12.

Perhaps the *Chambers* round about the temple, typefied what the Lord Jesus said:—

In my Father's house are many mansions.... I go to prepare a place for you. *John* xiv. 2.

The Temple of God was opened in heaven, and there was seen in His Temple the *Ark* of His testament. *Revelation* xi. 19.

I saw under the *Altar* the souls of them that were slain for the Word of God, and for the testimony which they held. *Rev.* vi. 9.

The *Cherubim* are represented by four beasts round about the throne:—

Which rest not day and night, saying, Holy, holy, holy, Lord God Almighty, which was, and is, and is to come. *Rev.* iv. 6-8. The four beasts and four and twenty elders fell down before the Lamb, having every one of them harps, and golden vials full of odours, [or incense,] which are the prayers of saints. *Rev.* v. 8.

And another angel came and stood at the altar, having a golden *censer*; and there was given unto him much incense, that he should offer it with the prayers of all saints upon the golden altar which was before the throne. *Rev.* viii. 3.

The *seven candlesticks* which thou sawest are the seven churches. *Rev.* i. 20. And there were *seven lamps* of fire burning before the throne, which are the seven spirits of God. *Rev.* iv. 5.

And I saw another sign in heaven, great and marvellous, seven angels having the seven last plagues; for in them is filled up the wrath of God. And I saw as it were a *sea of glass* mingled with fire: and them that had gotten the victory over the beast, and over his image, and over his mark, and over the number of his name, stand on the sea of glass, having the harps of God. And they sing the song of Moses the servant of God, and the song of the Lamb.... And after that I looked, and, behold, the temple of the tabernacle of the testimony in heaven was opened: And the seven angels came out of the temple, having the seven plagues, clothed in pure and *white linen*, and having their breasts girded with golden girdles. [The embroidered girdle of the ephod—the priest's garments shall be.... of gold, of blue, and purple, and scarlet, and fine twined linen. *Ex.* xxviii. 8.] And one of the four beasts gave unto the seven angels seven golden vials full of the wrath of God, who liveth for ever and ever. And the temple was filled with *smoke* from the Glory of God, and from His power. And no man was able to enter into the temple, till the seven plagues of the seven angels were fulfilled. *Rev.* xv.

So the Shekinah, the Glory of the Lord, had filled the Tabernacle and the Temple.

The molten sea held pure water to cleanse the priests before they ministered in the temple; so, perhaps, the sea of glass signifies the clear and transparent purity of the saints who have gotten the victory over sin, on which they stand in safety when the wrath of God is poured out upon the wicked.

The Ark of the Covenant, the Court of the Lord's house, the Chambers, the golden Altar, the Cherubim, the Censer and incense, the seven Candlesticks, the Sea of glass or the Laver, the holy Vestments, and the Shekinah, which were shown by the Spirit to Moses and to David as the pattern of the Sanctuary and all the instruments thereof, are thus revealed. Only the Vail is not seen in the heavenly city, for its type was fulfilled when, at the Lord's death, it was rent from the top to the bottom.

St. John also shows the true worship before the Throne, and the emblems of triumph over sin:-

I beheld, and, lo, a great multitude.... of all nations and kindreds, and people, and tongues, stood before the Throne, and before the Lamb, clothed with *white robes*, and *palms* in their hands; And cried with a loud voice, saying, Salvation to our God which sitteth upon the Throne, and unto the Lamb.... And one of the Elders answered, saying unto me, What are these which are arrayed in white robes? and whence came they? And I said unto him, Sir, thou knowest. And he said to me, These are they which came out of great tribulation, and have washed their robes, and made them white in the blood of the Lamb. Therefore are they before the throne of God, and serve Him day and night in His temple: and He that sitteth on the throne shall dwell among them. *Rev.* vii. 9-15.

The palms signified victory through righteousness, and were typefied by the palm trees carved on the doors of the Temple.

THE CHURCH MILITANT.

Isaiah says to the Church:—

Enlarge the place of thy *tent*, and let them stretch forth the *curtains* of thine habitations: spare not, lengthen thy cords, and strengthen thy stakes; For thou shalt break forth on the right hand and on the left; and thy seed shall inherit the Gentiles.... O thou afflicted, tossed with tempest, and not comforted, behold, I will lay thy stones with fair colours, and lay thy foundations with sapphires. And I will make thy windows of agates, and thy gates of carbuncles, and all thy borders of pleasant stones. *Is.* liv. 2-12.

This is evidently a simile borrowed from the Tabernacle and the Temple, by which the Church is encouraged to work on patiently, amid all discouragements. As the curtains and cords of the Tabernacle were enlarged into the Temple, so shall she be extended until she attain her glory.

The construction of the Church is thus described by David:—

Open to me the gates of righteousness; I will go into them, and I will praise the Lord; this *gate* of the Lord, into which the righteous shall enter. I will praise thee; for thou hast heard me, and art become my *salvation*. The *Stone* which the builders refused is become the head stone of the corner. *Ps.* cxviii. 19.

And St. Paul says:—

The head, even Christ: from whom the whole body *fitly joined together* and compacted by that which *every joint supplieth*, according to the effectual working in the measure of every part, maketh increase of the *body* unto the edifying of itself in love. *Eph.* iv. 15.

Christ is the head of the Church: and He is the Saviour of the body.... We are members of His body, of His flesh, and of His bones. *Eph.* v. 23, 30.

Here is the *Laver* through which we become members:—

By one Spirit we are all *baptized* into one body, whether we be Jews or Gentiles, whether we be bond or free; and have been all made to drink into one Spirit. For the body is not one member, but many... Now ye are the body of Christ, and members in particular. 1 *Cor.* 13, 14, 27.

Christ also loved the Church, and gave Himself for it; That He might sanctify and cleanse it with the *washing of water* by the Word. *Eph.* v. 25, 26.

Jesus answered, Verily, verily, I say unto thee, Except a man be *born of water* and of the Spirit, he cannot enter into the kingdom of God. *John* iii. 5.

Here is the *Temple*:—

What! know ye not that your body is the *temple* of the Holy Ghost which is in you, which ye have of God, and ye are not your own? 1 *Cor.* vi. 19.

This is the way this temple is to be built:—

Ye are God's building. According to the grace of God which is given unto me, as a wise masterbuilder, I have laid the foundation, and another buildeth thereon. But let every man take heed how he buildeth thereupon. For other foundation can no man lay than that is laid, which is Jesus Christ. Now if any man build upon this foundation *gold, silver, precious stones,* wood, hay, stubble; every man's work shall be made manifest: for the day shall declare it, because it shall be revealed by fire; and the fire shall try every man's work of what sort it is. 1 *Cor.* iii. 9–15.

Here are the *Priests* of this temple:—

Ye shall be named the priests of the Lord; men shall call you the ministers of our God. *Isaiah* lxi. 6.

But ye are a chosen generation, a royal priesthood, an holy nation, a peculiar people; that ye should shew forth the praises of Him who hath called you out of darkness into His marvellous light. 1 *Peter* ii. 9.

These are the *sacrifices* to be offered in this temple:—

The sacrifices of God are a broken spirit: a broken and a contrite heart, O God, thou wilt not despise. *Psalm* li. 17.

I beseech you therefore, brethren, by the mercies of God, that ye present your *bodies* a living sacrifice, holy, acceptable unto God, which is your reasonable service. *Rom.* xii. 1.

Dearly beloved, I beseech you as strangers and pilgrims, abstain from fleshly lusts, which war against the soul. 1 *Pet.* ii. 11.—Forasmuch as ye know that ye were not redeemed with corruptible things.... but with the precious blood of Christ, as of a lamb without blemish and without spot. 1 *Pet.* i. 18, 19.

We have an *Altar*, whereof they have no right to eat which serve the Tabernacle...... Jesus, that He might sanctify the people with His own blood, suffered without the gate.... By Him therefore let us offer the *sacrifice* of praise to God continually, that is, the fruit of our lips, giving thanks to His name. But to do good, and to communicate, forget not: for with such *sacrifices* God is well pleased. *Heb.* xiii. 10–16.

St. Paul says of the old dispensation:—

The priests went always into the first tabernacle, accomplishing the service of God. But into the second went the High Priest alone once every year, not without blood, which he offered for himself, and for the errors of the people: The Holy Ghost this signifying, that the *way* into the *holiest* of all was not yet made manifest, while as the first tabernacle was yet standing: Which was a *figure* for the time then present, in which were offered both gifts and sacrifices, that could not make him that did the service perfect, as pertaining to the conscience. *Heb.* ix. 6–9.

But the Lord Jesus says:—

I am the *way*, the truth, and the life: no man cometh unto the Father, but by me. *John* xiv. 6.

I am the *door*: by me if any man enter in, he shall be saved, and shall go in and out, and shall find pasture. *John* x. 9.

These are the *holy garments*:—

I will greatly rejoice in the Lord, my soul shall be joyful in my God; for He hath clothed me with the *garments of salvation*, He hath covered me with the *robe of righteousness*, as a bridegroom decketh himself with ornaments, and as a bride adorneth herself with jewels. *Isaiah* lxi. 10.

Here is the reappearance of the *Shekinah* in the Church: Jesus saith:—

I am come a *light* into the world, that whosoever believeth on me should not abide in darkness. *John* xii. 46.—And St. Paul says:—

God, who commanded the *light* to shine out of darkness, hath shined in our hearts, to give the light of the knowledge of the *glory* of God in the face of Jesus

Christ. 2 *Cor.* iv. 6.

The Lord thus warns us concerning the light of His Holy Spirit, that true Shekinah, which should ever shine in our hearts and lives:—

Take heed that the *light* which is in thee be not darkness. If thy whole body therefore be full of light, having no part dark, the whole shall be full of light, as when the bright shining of a *candle* doth give thee light. *Luke* xi. 35, 36.

When a person through the laying on of hands by the Bishop has been made a priest over his own body, which is now a "temple of the Holy Ghost," no one but the great High Priest can enter into the *most holy* place of his inmost heart. There he must continually offer the appointed sacrifices, that they who approach the *courts* of his outer life may perceive in him the *light* of the Spirit, and be illumined by his example. Such persons are good members of the body the Church, all fitly joined together to form the body of which Christ is the head and the corner stone.

For the Church of which this is the realization we are thus taught to pray in the second Collect for Good Friday:—

ALMIGHTY and everlasting God, by whose Spirit the whole body of the Church is governed and sanctified; receive our supplications and prayers, which we offer before thee for all estates of men in thy holy Church, that every member of the same, in his vocation and ministry, may truly and godly serve thee, through our Lord and Saviour Jesus Christ Amen.

CHAPTER XI.
HOLY JERUSALEM.

————:o:————

In both the Old and the New Testament the City of David, Jerusalem, and Mount Sion, are often used to typify the Church of the saints, the Lamb's Bride. St. Paul expressly speaks of the allegorical significance of Jerusalem:—

It is written, that Abraham had two sons; the one by a bond-maid, the other by a free-woman. But he who was of the bond-woman, was born after the flesh; but he of the free-woman was by promise. Which things are an *allegory*: for these are the two covenants; the one from the Mount Sinai, which gendereth to bondage, which is Agar. For this Agar is Mount Sinai in Arabia, and answereth to Jerusalem which now is, and is in bondage with her children. But Jerusalem which is above is free, which is the mother of us all. *Gal.* iv. 22–26.

David took [from the Jebusites] the stronghold of Zion: the same is the city of David. And in Jerusalem he reigned thirty and three years over Israel and Judah. 2 *Sam.* v. 7, 5.

After he had established his own house, David brought up the Ark of God from Gibeah to the city of David:—

And they brought in the Ark of the Lord and set it in his place, in the midst of the tabernacle that David had pitched for it. 2 *Sam.* vi.

The following are a few of the passages from the Psalms in which Zion and Jerusalem are spoken of:—

Great is the Lord, and greatly to be praised in the city of our God, in the mountain of His holiness. Beautiful for situation, the joy of the whole earth, is Mount Zion, on the sides of the North, the city of the great King. God is known in her palaces for a refuge.... As we have heard, so have we seen in the city of the Lord of hosts, in the city of our God: God will establish it for ever. *Psalm* xlviii. 1-8.

Do good in thy good pleasure unto Zion: build thou the walls of Jerusalem. Then shalt thou be pleased with the sacrifices of righteousness. *Ps.* li. 18, 19.

Our feet shall stand within thy gates, O Jerusalem. Jerusalem is builded as a city that is compact together: whither the tribes go up, the tribes of the Lord unto the testimony of Israel, to give thanks unto the name of the Lord. For there are set thrones of judgment, the thrones of the house of David. Pray for the peace of Jerusalem: they shall prosper that love thee. Peace be within thy walls, and prosperity within thy palaces. *Psalm* cxxii.

Blessed be the Lord out of Zion, which dwelleth at Jerusalem. *Psalm* cxxxv. 21.

His foundation is in the Holy Mountains. The Lord loveth the gates of Zion more than all the dwellings of Jacob. *Psalm* lxxxvii. 1, 2.

The "gates of Zion" undoubtedly refer to those beautiful gates of "that great city, the holy Jerusalem," seen by St. John. *Rev.* xxi.

The expression "The Lord loveth the gates of *Zion* more than all the dwellings of Jacob," is peculiar. What does it mean? Is it possible that the Lord loves the ways of one particular church which in all things conforms strictly to the teaching of His Word, more than He does those of others which believe in Him, and yet in some matters choose their own interpretation of the Word? Are the "dwellings of Jacob" like the "little ships" which were with Him, while He was in *the* ship?

The Lord hath chosen Zion: He hath *desired* it for His habitation. This is my rest for ever: here will I dwell; for I have desired it. *Psalm* cxxxii. 13, 14.

Let Israel rejoice in Him that made him: let the children of Zion be joyful in their King. *Ps.* cxlix. 2.

David thus more distinctly prophesies of Him who is the Head of the Church:—

Yet have I set my King upon my holy hill of Zion. I will declare the decree: the Lord hath said unto me, Thou art my Son; this day have I begotten thee. *Ps.* ii. 6, 7.—*Acts* xiii. 33.—*Heb.* i. 5.

The Lord said unto my Lord, Sit thou at my right hand, until I make thine enemies thy footstool. The Lord shall send the rod of thy strength out of Zion: rule thou in the midst of thine enemies. *Ps.* cx. 1, 2.

The Prophets also use the same figurative language in reference to the Church of God:—

The Lord hath founded Zion, and the poor of His people shall trust in it. *Isaiah* xiv. 32.

The ransomed of the Lord shall return, and come to *Zion* with songs, and everlasting joy upon their heads: they shall obtain joy and gladness, and sorrow and sighing shall flee away. *Is.* xxxv. 10.

O Zion, that bringest good tidings, get thee up into the *high mountain*: O Jerusalem, that bringest good tidings, lift up thy voice with strength; lift it up, be not afraid; say unto the cities of Judah, Behold your God.... He shall feed His flock like a shepherd. *Is.* xl. 3, 9, 11.

The "high mountain" is the Church, of which

Isaiah and Micah prophesy:—

It shall come to pass in the last days, that the *mountain* of the Lord's house shall be established in the top of the mountains, and shall be exalted above the hills; and all nations shall flow unto it. And many people shall go and say, Come ye, and let us go up to the mountain of the Lord, to the house of the God of Jacob; and He will teach us of His ways, and we will walk in His paths: for out of Zion shall go forth the law, and the Word of the Lord from Jerusalem. *Is.* ii. 2, 3.–*Micah* iv. 1, 2.

And the Redeemer shall come to Zion, and unto them that turn from transgression in Jacob, saith the Lord. *Is.* lix. 20.

St. Paul thus quotes this passage:—

As it is written, There shall come out of Sion the Deliverer, and shall turn away ungodliness from Jacob. *Romans* xi. 26.

Awake, awake; put on thy strength, O Zion; put on thy beautiful garments, O Jerusalem, the holy city.... How beautiful upon the mountains are the feet of him that bringeth good tidings, that publisheth peace; that bringeth good tidings of good, that publisheth salvation; that sayeth unto Zion, Thy God reigneth. *Isaiah* lii. 1, 7.

The glory of Lebanon shall come unto thee.... They shall call thee, The city of the Lord, the Zion of the Holy One of Israel.... and thou shalt know that I the Lord am thy Saviour, and thy Redeemer, the mighty One of Jacob.... Thou shalt call thy walls Salvation, and thy gates Praise. The sun shall be no more thy light by day.... but the Lord shall be unto thee an everlasting light, and thy God thy glory. *Is.* lx. 13–19.

St. John specially applies this prophecy to the

Lamb's Wife. *Rev.* xxi. 23.

St. Paul writes in the same strain to the Jews, and applies these predictions of the Redeemer, the Deliverer, the Saviour, and the King, to the Lord Jesus:—

But ye are come unto Mount Sion, and unto the city of the living God, the heavenly Jerusalem, and to an innumerable company of angels, To the general assembly and church of the firstborn, which are written in heaven, and to God the Judge of all, and to the spirits of just men made perfect, And to Jesus the Mediator of the new covenant, and to the blood of sprinkling, that speaketh better things than that of Abel. *Heb.* xii. 22–24.

In accordance with this allegorical teaching, our Lord and Saviour offered Himself as the great sacrifice of atonement *at Jerusalem*, fulfilling the type of the Passover. After His resurrection, He opened the understandings of His Apostles:—

That they might understand the Scriptures, and said unto them, Thus it is written, and thus it behoved Christ to suffer, and to rise from the dead the third day: And that repentance and remission of sins should be preached in His name among all nations, *beginning at Jerusalem. Luke* xxiv. 45–47.

And He commanded them:—

Tarry ye in the city of Jerusalem, until ye be endued with power from on high. *Luke* xxiv. 49.

It was in Jerusalem that the Apostles received the Holy Ghost, (*Acts* i. 11.) and "*Strangers of Rome*" were there, and heard them speak in their own tongue. *Acts* ii. 10.

It was in Jerusalem that they began to work miracles and to preach, causing many to believe.

It was in Jerusalem that they chose the seven deacons:—

And when they had prayed, they laid their hands on them. And the word of God increased; and the number of the disciples multiplied in Jerusalem greatly; and a great company of the Priests were obedient to the faith. *Acts* vi. 1–7.

It was in Jerusalem that the protomartyr, St. Stephen, was put to death because he testified to the truth as it is in Jesus. *Acts* vii.

When certain of the disciples went out as missionaries to the Gentiles in other places:—

The hand of the Lord was with them: and a great number believed, and turned unto the Lord. Then tidings of these things came unto the ears of the Church which was in Jerusalem: and they sent forth Barnabas. *Acts* xi. 21, 22.

When a grave question under the Jewish law arose among the disciples who were establishing the Church at Antioch:—

They determined that Paul and Barnabas and certain of them, should go up to Jerusalem, unto the Apostles and elders, about this question.... And when they were come to Jerusalem, they were received of the Church, and of the Apostles and elders; and they declared all things that God had done with them.... And the Apostles and elders came together, for to consider of this matter.

After discussion, St. James as presiding Bishop, pronounced his sentence; and that judgment was sent out to Antioch as that which seemed good to the Holy Ghost and to them. *Acts* xv.

From this it appears that the first Council of the Church was held at Jerusalem.

After these things the chief rulers of the Jews conspired to kill Paul at Jerusalem, and he was protected against them in the castle by the Roman soldiers.

And the night following, the Lord stood by him, and said, Be of good cheer, Paul: for as thou hast testified of me in Jerusalem, so must thou bear witness also at *Rome*. *Acts* xxiii. 11.

Paul, having appealed to Cæsar, was taken to Rome. There he called together the chief of the Jews, and explained to them the cause of his arrest. And the Jews in Rome said unto him:—

We neither received letters out of Judæa concerning thee, neither any of the brethren that came shewed or spake any harm of thee. But we desire to hear of thee what thou thinkest: for as concerning this sect, we know that every where it is spoken against. And when they had appointed him a day, there came many to him into his lodging; to whom he expounded and testified the kingdom of God, persuading them concerning Jesus, both out of the law of Moses, and out of the prophets, from morning till evening. And some believed the things which were spoken, and some believed not. *Acts* xxviii. 17–24.

So one went from the Apostles and elders at Jerusalem to teach the doctrines of the Church to the people at Rome.

Must we explain away all this allegorical and historical teaching concerning the Church "built upon the Apostles and Prophets, Jesus Christ Himself being the chief corner stone," and substitute for the Church beginning at Jerusalem, a church beginning at Rome? Does the Church of Rome, with all her traditions, fulfil the type of

Jerusalem the mother of us all? For many years she sought by inciting the Crusades, to gain permanent possession of Jerusalem which now is. Had she succeeded she might have established there her "infallible" See. The fact that all attempts to wrest Jerusalem from the Moslems have failed, seems to indicate that the allegory was not thus to be realized. The Temple was destroyed, and its Court given over to the Gentiles to be trodden under foot by them, perhaps to show that the sacrifices were no longer to be offered in any particular place, but that the Father should be worshipped, as Jesus told the woman of Samaria, "Neither in this mountain, nor yet at Jerusalem," but "In spirit and in truth: For the Father seeketh such to worship Him." *John* iv. 21-24.

In the Collect for St. Mark's Day we are thus taught to pray:—

O ALMIGHTY God, who hast instructed thy holy Church with the heavenly doctrine of thy Evangelist Saint Mark; give us grace, that being not like children carried away with every blast of vain doctrine, we may be established in the truth of thy holy Gospel, through Jesus Christ our Lord. *Amen.*

CHAPTER XII.

THE KING OF ISRAEL.

—:o:—

In uttering the words, "I gave thee a king in mine anger and took him away in my wrath," (*Hosea* xiii. 11.) the Prophet probably alludes immediately to Saul as the king; but he may have had prophetically a far grander meaning.

When Samuel was old...... all the elders of Israel gathered themselves together, and came to Samuel unto Ramah, and said unto him, Behold, thou art old and thy sons walk not in thy ways: now make us a *king* to *judge* us like all the nations. But the thing displeased Samuel.... And Samuel prayed unto the Lord. And the Lord said unto Samuel, Hearken unto the voice of the people in all that they say unto thee: for they have not rejected thee, but they have rejected Me, that I should not reign over them. 1 *Samuel* viii. 1–7.—Then Samuel warned the people that their king would oppress and despoil them.

Nevertheless, the people refused to obey the voice of Samuel: and they said, Nay; but we will have a king over us; that we also may be like all the nations; and that our king may *judge* us, and go out before us, and fight our battles. 1 *Samuel* viii.

Then Samuel rebuked the people, telling them how often the Lord had delivered them from their enemies; yet they insisted that they would have a king to reign over them, when the Lord their God was their King. 1 *Samuel* xii.

Accordingly, the Lord caused Saul, an ideal warrior and leader after the fancy of the people, to be chosen king, and Samuel anointed him king over Israel.

And Samuel said to all the people, See ye him whom the Lord hath chosen, that there is none like him among all the people? And all the people shouted and said, God save the king! 1 *Samuel* x. 24.

But Saul offended the Lord in doing wickedly, and in oppressing the people. So, when war was raging with the Philistines:—

The battle went sore against Saul, and the archers hit him; and he was sore wounded of the archers.... therefore Saul took a sword and fell upon it...... So Saul died, and his three sons. 1 *Samuel* xxxi. 1–6.

Thus God "took away in his wrath" this king whom He had given Israel "in His anger."

About 350 years after Saul's death, the Lord by His prophet said:—

I will be thy King: where is any other that may save thee in all thy cities and thy *judges*, of whom thou saidst, Give me a king and princes?.... I will ransom them from the power of the grave, I will redeem them from death: O death, I will be thy plagues; O grave, I will be thy destruction. *Hos.* xiii. 10, 14.

This is a distinct prophecy of "JESUS OF NAZARETH THE KING OF THE JEWS;" (*John* xix. 19.) of whom St. Paul, in the portion of Scripture appointed by the Church to be read in "The order for the burial of the dead," says:—

O death, where is thy sting? O grave, where is thy victory? The sting of death is sin; and the strength of sin is the law. But thanks be to God, which giveth us the victory through our Lord Jesus Christ. 1 *Cor.* xv. 55–57.

Through a long course of years the kings of Judah and of Israel led their people to commit frightful sins, until at length God brought upon them all the judgments which He had threatened by prophets, judges, and seers, to induce them to turn away from their iniquities.

Then God once more offered Himself to them as their King. In His infinite love He sent His only Son to them. He came in the form of a man

having by regular descent the legal right to reign over them; for as Calmet shows from the two genealogies in Matthew i, and Luke iii, His mother Mary was the daughter of Heli, who was descended from David through Nathan; and His reputed father Joseph was likewise descended from David through Solomon. But, again failing to apprehend the divine purpose of their King, which was to give them everlasting life, they rejected Him:—
But they cried out, Away with Him, away with Him crucify Him. Pilate saith unto them, Shall I crucify your King? The Chief Priests answered, We have no king but Cæsar. *John* xix. 15.

And now came the fulfilment of Jacob's prophecy (*Gen.* xlix. 10.) "The Sceptre shall not depart from Judah, nor a lawgiver from between his feet until Shiloh come." Shiloh—He whose right it is— as says Ezekiel:—
Exalt Him that is low, and abase him that is high. I will overturn, overturn, overturn it: and it shall be no more, until He come *whose right it is*: and I will give it Him. *Ezek.* xxi. 26, 27.

Since the Jews rejected Jesus of Nazareth for their King, the Lord God hath taken away the sceptre from their nation. They have no civil ruler, judge, or lawgiver of their own, but are subject to those of the nations among whom they are dispersed. Thus God hath taken away their king in His wrath, because they rejected Him that He should not reign over them. It seems to be with a purpose that this passage from Hosea is appointed by the Church to be read on the second Sunday of the Easter season.

As if to teach us our duty to have charity towards the Jews, the Lord prayed for them while they crucified Him: "Father forgive them; for they know not what they do." (*Luke* xxiii. 34.) So, in commemorating His precious death on each Good Friday, the Church thus prays for them:—

O MERCIFUL God, who hast made all men, and hatest nothing that thou hast made, nor desirest the death of a sinner, but rather that he should be converted and live; have mercy upon all Jews.... and take from them all ignorance, hardness of heart, and contempt of thy word; and so fetch them home, blessed Lord, to thy flock, that they may be saved among the remnant of the true Israelites, and be made one fold under one Shepherd, Jesus Christ our Lord, who liveth and reigneth with thee and the Holy Spirit, one God, world without end. *Amen.*

CHAPTER XIII.

THE WORD.

———:o:———

As the purpose of the Bible is to make known to man the Lord Jesus Christ, the author of salvation, we may naturally expect that the Word of which we so often read, may sometimes mean that very "WORD" who was made flesh and dwelt among us.

Moses thus begins his record of the Creation:—
In the beginning God created the heaven and the earth. *Gen.* i. 1.

And David says:—
By the Word of the Lord were the heavens made; and all the host of them by the Breath of His mouth.

Psalm xxxiii. 6.—St. John says:—

In the beginning was the Word, and the Word was with God, and the Word *was* GOD.... All things were made by Him; and without Him was not anything made that was made. He was in the world, and the world was made by Him. *John* i. 1-10.

And St. Paul declares:—

Through faith we understand that the worlds were formed by the WORD OF GOD, so that things which are seen were not made of things which do appear.

Heb. xi. 3.—By the same faith we may understand other passages relating to the Word.

While Samuel was yet a child:—

The Word of the Lord was precious, there was no open vision...... Samuel did not yet know the Lord, neither was the Word of the Lord yet revealed unto him. 1 *Sam.* iii. 1, 7.

But the Lord called to Samuel and told him what He would do to the house of Eli.

And Samuel grew, and the Lord was with him.... And all Israel knew that Samuel was established to be a prophet of the Lord. And the Lord appeared again in Shiloh: for the Lord revealed Himself to Samuel in Shiloh by the Word of the Lord. 1 *Sam.* iii.

After the Angel of the Lord had appeared to him as he lay under the juniper tree, Elijah went:

Unto Horeb the mount of God. And he came thither unto a cave, and lodged there; and, behold, the Word of the Lord came to him, and He said unto him, What doest thou here, Elijah?

Then came the wind, and the earthquake, and the fire:

And after the fire a still small voice...... And the Lord said unto him, Go, return on thy way to the wilderness of Damascus: and when thou comest, anoint Hazael to be king over Syria. 1 *Kings* xix. 4-15.

Here the Word is alluded to as a person–*He* said unto him.

David says:–

Remember the Word unto thy servant, upon which thou hast caused me to hope.... They that fear thee will be glad when they see me; because I have hoped in thy Word.... This is my comfort in my affliction: for thy Word hath *quickened* me. *Ps.* cxix. 46-74.

But the Lord Jesus saith:–

As the Father raiseth up the dead, and *quickeneth* them; even so the Son quickeneth whom He will. *John* v. 21.—And St. Paul says:–

The first man Adam was made a living soul; the last Adam [Christ] was made a *quickening* Spirit. 1 *Cor.* xv. 45.—David says:–

Thy Word is a *lamp* unto my feet, and a *light* unto my path. *Psalm* cxix. 105.

And Isaiah thus predicts the Saviour:–

For Zion's sake will I not hold my peace, and for Jerusalem's sake I will not rest, until the righteousness thereof go forth as brightness, and the *Salvation* thereof as a *lamp* that burneth. And the Gentiles shall see thy righteousness. *Isaiah* lxii. 1, 2.

St. Luke says of the Lord Jesus:–

For so hath the Lord commanded us, saying, I have set Thee to be a *light* of the Gentiles, that Thou shouldest be for *salvation* unto the ends of the earth. And when the Gentiles heard this, they were glad, and glorified the Word of the Lord: and as many as were ordained to eternal life believed. And the Word of the Lord was published throughout all the region. *Acts* xiii. 47-49.

And St. Peter declares:-

We have also a more sure Word of prophecy; whereunto ye do well that ye take heed, as unto a *light* that shineth in a dark place, until the day dawn, and the day Star arise in your hearts. *2 Peter* i. 19.

David says:-

I will worship toward thy holy temple, and praise thy name for thy loving kindness and for thy truth: for thou hast magnified thy WORD above all thy name. *Psalm* cxxxviii. 2.—And St. Paul says:-

That the God of our Lord Jesus Christ, the Father of glory, may give unto you the spirit of wisdom and revelation in the knowledge of Him...... which He wrought in Christ, when He raised Him from the dead, and set Him at His own right hand in the heavenly places, far above all principality, and power, and might, and *every name* that is named, not only in this world, but also in that which is to come. *Eph.* i. 17.

And again he says:-

Wherefore God also hath highly exalted Him, and given Him [Christ] a *Name* which is *above every name*: That at the Name of JESUS every knee should bow, of things in heaven, and things in earth, and things under the earth. *Phil.* ii. 9, 10.

But the Prophet Isaiah says:-

Look unto me and be ye saved, all the ends of the earth; for I am GOD, and there is none else. I have sworn by myself, the Word is gone out of my mouth in righteousness, and shall not return, That unto me every knee shall bow, every tongue shall swear. *Is.* xlv. 22, 23.—David says:-

For ever, O Lord, thy Word is settled in heaven. *Psalm* cxix. 89.—And Isaiah says:-

The voice of him that crieth in the wilderness, Prepare ye the way of the Lord, make straight in the desert a highway for our God.... The voice said, Cry .... the grass withereth, the flower fadeth: but the Word of our God shall stand *for ever*. *Is.* xl. 3-8.

St. Peter quoting Isaiah says:—

Love one another with a pure heart fervently: being born again, not of corruptible seed, but of incorruptible, by the Word of God which *liveth* and abideth *for ever*. For all flesh is as grass, and all the glory of man as the flower of grass. The grass withereth, and the flower thereof falleth away: but the Word of the Lord endureth *for ever*. And this is the WORD which by the Gospel is preached unto you. 1 *Pet.* i. 22-25.

This is He of whom it is written:—

Of His own will begat He us with the Word of truth, that we should be a kind of first fruits of His creatures. *James* i. 18.

The Lord Jesus saith:—

Holy Father, keep through thine own name those whom Thou hast given me.... Sanctify them through thy truth: thy Word is truth. *John* xvii. 11, 17.

Jesus saith, I am the truth. *John* xiv. 6.

Again, St. Paul says:—

Christ also loved the Church, and gave Himself for it; That He might *sanctify* and cleanse it with the washing of water by the Word. *Eph.* v. 25, 26.

But of Him are ye in Christ Jesus, who of God is made unto us wisdom, and righteousness, and *sanctification*, and redemption. 1 *Cor.* i. 30.

St. Paul says:—

The Word of God is quick, and powerful, and sharper than any twoedged sword, piercing even to the dividing asunder of the joints and marrow, and is a discerner of the thoughts and intents of the heart. *Heb.* iv.

While St. John declares of Him whose "Name is called the WORD OF GOD:"—

Out of His mouth goeth a sharp sword, that with it He should smite the nations: and He shall rule them with a rod of iron...... And He hath on His vesture and on His thigh a name written, King of kings, and Lord of lords. *Rev.* xix. 13–16.

St. John explicitly declares:—

The Word was God...... and the Word was made flesh, and dwelt among us, (and we beheld His glory, the glory as of the only begotten of the Father,) full of grace and truth. *John* i. 1, 14.

And again, he speaks of:—

That which was in the beginning, which we have heard, which we have seen with our eyes, which we have looked upon, and our hands have handled, of the Word of life. 1 *John* i. 1.

Of this Word of God St. Paul testifies:—

Men and brethren, children of the stock of Abraham and whosoever feareth God, to you is the Word of this salvation sent. For they that dwell at Jerusalem, and their rulers, because they knew Him not, nor yet the voices of the prophets which are read every Sabbath day, they have fulfilled them in condemning Him. *Acts* xiii. 26, 27.

In this sense the Church uses the Word in connection with the Father and the Holy Spirit, when in the Invocation, during the Administration of the Holy Communion, the Minister says:—

And we most humbly beseech thee, O merciful Father, to hear us; and of thy almighty goodness, vouchsafe to bless and sanctify, with thy Word and Holy Spirit, these thy gifts and creatures of bread and wine; that we, receiving them according to thy Son our Saviour Jesus Christ's holy institution, in remembrance of His death and passion, may be partakers of His most blessed Body and Blood.

The Collect for the Second Sunday in Advent teaches us to say :—

BLESSED Lord, who hast caused all holy Scriptures to be written for our learning; grant that we may in such wise hear them, read, mark, learn, and inwardly digest them, that by patience and comfort of thy holy Word, we may embrace, and ever hold fast the blessed hope of everlasting life, which thou hast given us in our Saviour Jesus Christ. *Amen.*

CHAPTER XIV.

THE ANGEL OF THE LORD.

———:o:———

Angel means, *one sent*, or, a messenger. There is reason to believe that God sent His own Son under the name of "The Angel of the Lord," to accomplish His loving purposes towards man, before He appeared "in the likeness of sinful flesh," before "The Word was made flesh, and dwelt among us." He likewise appears in the Scripture as a Man, and as The Captain of the host of the Lord. In the passages which describe such visitations of the Son, the Angel speaks "as one having authority," without the announcement, "Thus saith the Lord."

St. Paul says:—

What the law could not do, in that it was weak through the flesh, God *sending* His own Son in the likeness of sinful flesh, and for sin, condemned sin in the flesh. *Rom.* viii. 3.

When Hagar, Sarai's maid, fled from the face of her mistress:—

The Angel of the Lord found her by a fountain of water in the wilderness...... And the Angel of the Lord said unto her, *I will* multiply thy seed exceedingly, that it should not be numbered for multitude... And she called the name of the *Lord* that spake unto her, Thou GOD seest me: for she said, Have I also here looked after Him that seeth me. *Gen.* xvi. 7-13.

Jacob told his wives Leah and Rachel:—

The Angel of God spake unto me in a dream, saying, I AM the God of Beth-el, where thou anointedst the pillar, and where thou vowedst a vow unto me. *Gen.* xxxi. 11, 13.

Hosea says of Jacob, in reference to his wrestling with the *Man* at the ford Jabbok:—

By his strength he had power with God: Yea, he had power over the Angel, and prevailed: he wept, and made supplications unto Him: he found Him in Beth-el, and there He spake with us; Even the Lord God of hosts; the Lord is His memorial. *Hos.* xii. 3-5.

There was a certain man of Zorah, of the family of the Danites, whose name was Manoah; and his wife was barren, and bare not. And the Angel of the Lord appeared unto the woman, and said unto her, Thou shalt bear a son.... Then the woman came and told her husband, saying, A man of God came unto me, and His countenance was like the countenance of an Angel of God, very terrible: but I asked Him not whence He was, neither told He me His name... Then Manoah entreated the Lord, and said, O my Lord, let the man of God which Thou didst *send* come again unto us, and teach us what we shall do unto the child that shall be born. And God hearkened to the voice of Manoah; and the Angel of God came again to the woman as she sat in the field: but Manoah her husband was not with her. And the woman made haste and ran, and shewed her husband, and said unto him, Behold, the man hath appeared unto me, that came unto me the other day. And Manoah arose, and went after his wife, and came to the man, and said unto him, Art thou the Man that spakest unto the woman? And He said, I AM...... And the Angel of the Lord said unto Manoah, Of all that I said unto the woman let her beware.... And Manoah said unto the Angel of the Lord, What is thy Name, that when thy sayings come to pass we may do thee honour? And the Angel of the Lord said unto him, Why askest thou thus after my Name, seeing it is secret [or, wonderful. *Marg.*]? So Manoah took a kid with a meat offering, and offered it on a rock unto the Lord: and the Angel did *wonderously*; and Manoah and his wife looked on. For it came to pass, when the flame went up toward heaven from off the altar, that the Angel of the Lord ascended in the flame of the altar.... Then Manoah knew that He was an Angel of the Lord. And Manoah said unto his wife, We shall surely die because we have seen God. *Judges.* xiii.

Predicting the Son of God, Isaiah says:-

Unto us a child is born, unto us a Son is given: and the government shall be upon His shoulder: and His Name shall be called *Wonderful*. *Isaiah* ix. 6.

When Israel was oppressed by the Midianites:-

The Lord sent a prophet unto the children of Israel, which said unto them, Thus saith the Lord God of Israel, I brought you up from Egypt.

Immediately after we read:—

And there came an Angel of the Lord.... and appeared unto Gideon, and said unto him, The Lord is with thee, thou mighty man of valour...... And the *Lord* looked upon him, and said, Go in this thy might, and thou shalt save Israel from the hand of the Midianites: have not *I sent* thee?.... And Gideon went in, and made ready a kid, and unleavened cakes...... and the Angel of God said unto him, Take the flesh and the unleavened cakes, and lay them upon this rock.... Then the Angel of the Lord put forth the end of the staff that was in His hand and touched the flesh and the unleavened cakes; and there rose up fire out of the rock, and consumed the flesh and the unleavened cakes. Then the Angel of the Lord departed out of his sight. And when Gideon perceived that He was an Angel of the Lord, Gideon said, Alas, O Lord God! for because I have seen an Angel of the Lord face to face. And the Lord said unto him, Peace be unto thee; fear not: thou shalt not die. *Judges* vi.

While the Prophet coming with his message, says, Thus saith the Lord, the Angel says, Have not I sent thee.

During the delivery of the Law on Mount Sinai, the Lord said to Moses:—

Behold, I send an Angel before thee, to keep thee in the way, and to bring thee into the place which I have prepared. Beware of Him, and obey His voice, provoke Him not; for He will not *pardon* your transgressions: for My Name is in Him. *Ex.* xxiii. 20, 21.

This is very like the command of the Father:—
This is my beloved Son: hear Him. *Luke* ix. 35.

When Balak sent word to Balaam to come and curse Israel:—

God came unto Balaam at night, and said unto him, If the men come to call thee, rise up, and go with them; but yet the word which I shall say unto thee, that shalt thou do.

As he went, the Angel of the Lord withstood him in the way three times.

Then the Lord opened the eyes of Balaam, and he saw the Angel of the Lord standing in the way, and His sword drawn in His hand: And he bowed down his head and fell flat on his face. And the Angel of the Lord said unto him...... I went out to withstand thee, because thy way is perverse before me.... And Balaam said unto the Angel of the Lord, I have sinned; for I knew not that thou stoodest in the way against me: now therefore, if it displease thee, I will get me back again. And the Angel of the Lord said unto Balaam, Go with the men: but only the word *that I shall speak* unto thee, that thou shalt speak.... And Balaam said unto Balak.... the word that *God putteth in my mouth*, that shall I speak. *Ex.* xxii.

It came to pass, when Joshua was by Jericho, that he lifted up his eyes and looked, and, behold, there stood a *Man* over against him with His *sword drawn* in his hand: and Joshua went unto Him, and said unto Him, Art thou for us, or for our adversaries? And He said, Nay; but as *Captain of the host of the Lord* am I now come. And Joshua fell on his face to the earth, and did worship, and said unto Him, What saith my Lord unto His servant? And the Captain of the Lord's host said unto Joshua, Loose thy shoe from off thy foot: for the place whereon thou standest is holy. And Joshua did so. *Josh.* v. 13-15.

David says:—

The chariots of God are twenty thousand, even

thousands of angels: the Lord is among them, as in Sinai, in the holy place. *Psalm* lxviii. 17.

And St. Paul says:—

The Lord Jesus shall be revealed from heaven with His mighty angels, in flaming fire taking vengeance on them that know not God, and that obey not the gospel of our Lord Jesus Christ. 2 *Thess.* i. 7, 8.

But while the Lord Jesus, who is called the Captain of our salvation, (*Heb.* ii. 10.) will lead His host to destroy His enemies, to those who love and serve Him He says, as Elisha said to his servant when the Syrians compassed them:—

Fear not: for they that be with us are more than they that be with them. And Elisha prayed and said Lord, I pray thee, open his eyes, that he may see. And the Lord opened the eyes of the young man; and he saw and, behold, the mountain was full of horses and chariots of fire round about Elisha. 2 *Kings* vi.

David says:—

The Angel of the Lord encampeth round about them that fear Him, and delivereth them. *Ps.* xxxiv. 7.

An Angel of the Lord came up from Gilgal to Bochim, and said, I made you to go up out of Egypt, and have brought you into the land which I sware unto your fathers; and I said, I will never break my covenant with you. *Judges* ii. 1.

God spake all these words, saying, I am the Lord thy God, which have brought thee out of the land of Egypt. *Exodus* xx. 1, 2.

The *Lord* said unto Abram, I will establish my *covenant* between me and thee and thy seed after thee in their generations for an everlasting covenant, to be a God unto thee. *Gen.* xvii. 1, 7.

In reading these and other similar passages

"written for our learning," we may pray for the benefit to be derived from them, in the words of the Collect for The Annunciation of the Blessed Virgin Mary (*Luke* i. 26–38.) :–

WE beseech thee, O Lord, pour thy grace into our hearts; that as we have known the incarnation of thy Son Jesus Christ by the message of an angel; so by His cross and passion we may be brought unto the glory of His resurrection, through the same Jesus Christ our Lord. *Amen.*

CHAPTER XV.

THE ROCK–THE STONE.

———:o:———

The many allusions in the Old Testament to God and to the Lord as the Rock and the Stone, are shown by parallel passages of the New Testament to refer to the Lord Jesus Christ:–

Moses says:–

Ascribe ye greatness unto our God. He is the Rock. *Deut.* xxxii. 3, 4.

But Jeshurun...... forsook God which made him, and lightly esteemed the Rock of his salvation.... Of the Rock that begat thee thou art unmindful, and hast forgotten God that formed thee. *Deut.* xxxii. 15.

David says:–

The Lord is my Rock, and my fortress, and my deliverer; my God.... the horn of my salvation.... For who is God save the Lord? or who is a Rock save our God? *Psalm* xviii. 2, 31.

Truly my soul waiteth upon God: from Him cometh

my salvation.... He only is my Rock and my salvation. *Psalm* lxii. 1–7.

Isaiah says:–

Sanctify the Lord of hosts Himself; and let Him be your fear.... And He shall be for a sanctuary; but for a Stone of stumbling, and for a Rock of offence to both the houses of Israel, for a gin and for a snare to the inhabitants of Jerusalem. *Isaiah* viii. 13, 14.

St. Paul thus explains this text:–

The Gentiles, which followed not after righteousness, have attained to righteousness, even the righteousness which is of faith. But Israel, which followed after the law of righteousness, hath not attained to the law of righteousness. Wherefore? Because they sought it not by *faith*, but as it were by the works of the law. For they stumbled at that stumbling-stone; As it is written, Behold, I lay in Sion a stumbling-stone and Rock of offence: and whosoever believeth on Him shall not be ashamed. *Rom.* ix.30–33.

When Simon Peter confessed the Lord and said:–

Thou art the Christ, the Son of the living God, Jesus answered and said unto him.... flesh and blood hath not revealed it unto thee, but my Father which is in heaven.... upon this Rock I will build my Church; and the gates of hell shall not prevail against it. *Matt.* xvi. 16–18.

St. Peter does not claim that himself is the Rock upon whom the Lord would build His Church when he quotes the Scripture:–

Behold, I lay in Sion a chief Corner-Stone, elect, precious: and he that believeth on Him shall not be confounded. 1 *Peter* ii. 6.

St. Peter having healed the impotent man, said to the Rulers and Elders:–

Be it known unto you all, and to all the people, of Israel, that by the Name of Jesus Christ of Nazareth, whom ye crucified, whom God raised from the dead, even by Him doth this man stand here before you whole. This is the Stone which was set at nought of you builders, which is become the head of the corner. Neither is there salvation in any other: for there is none other name under heaven given among men, whereby we must be saved. *Acts* iv. 8–12.

The foundation Stone is shown in what the Lord said in ending His sermon on the Mount:—

Whosoever heareth these sayings of mine, and doeth them, I will liken him unto a wise man, which built his house upon a *rock*: And the rain descended, and the floods came, and the winds blew, and beat upon that house; and it fell not: for it was founded upon a rock. *Matt.* vii. 24, 25.

There is a fine allegory in the stories of the Rock at Horeb and Kadesh.

All the congregation of the Children of Israel journeyed from the wilderness of Sin.... and pitched in Rephidim: and there was no water for the people to drink. Wherefore the people did chide with Moses, and said, Give us water that we may drink.... And Moses cried unto the Lord, saying, What shall I do unto this people? they be almost ready to stone me. And the Lord said unto Moses, Go on before the people, and take with thee of the elders of Israel; and thy rod, wherewith thou smotest the river, take in thine hand, and go. Behold, I will stand before thee there upon the Rock in Horeb; and thou shalt *smite* the Rock, and there shall come water out of it, that the people may drink. And Moses did so in the sight of the elders of Israel. *Exodus* xvii. 1–6.

In this case Moses is told to *smite* the rock.

Then came the children of Israel.... into the desert of Zin in the first month: and the people abode in Kadesh.... And there was no water for the congregation: and they gathered themselves together against Moses and against Aaron. And the people chode with Moses...... And the Lord spake unto Moses, saying, Take thy rod, and gather thou the assembly together, thou, and Aaron thy brother, and *speak* ye unto the rock before their eyes; and it shall give forth his water.... And Moses took the rod from before the Lord, as He commanded him. And Moses and Aaron gathered the congregation together before the rock, and he said unto them, Hear now, ye rebels; must we fetch you water out of this rock? And Moses lifted up his hand, and with his rod he *smote* the rock twice: and the water came out abundantly, and the congregation drank, and their beasts also. And the Lord spake unto Moses and Aaron, because ye believed me not, to sanctify me in the eyes of the children of Israel, therefore ye shall not bring this Congregation into the land which I have given them. *Num.* xx. 1-12.

Here the Lord's command was "*Speak* ye unto the rock;" and He was displeased with Moses and Aaron because in their anger they failed to fulfil the purpose of His command, and *smote* the rock instead of only speaking to it.

That this, though a true story, is also an allegory may be inferred from what St. Paul says:—

Brethren, I would not that ye should be ignorant, how that all our fathers.... did all eat the same spiritual meat; And did all drink the same spiritual drink: for they drank of that spiritual Rock that followed them: and that Rock was Christ. 1 *Cor.* x. 1-4.

The Lord Jesus Himself says:—

Whosoever drinketh of the water that I shall give him shall never thirst; but the water that I shall give him shall be in him a well of water springing up into everlasting life. *John* iv. 14.

But this spake He of the Spirit which they that believe on Him should receive. *John* vii. 39.

This then is the solution of the allegory which Moses would have seen had not his faith been dimmed by anger with the people. He did not believe—that is, fully apprehend—the intent of the Lord: so he failed to sanctify the Lord in the eyes of the children of Israel, and was punished in not being permitted to lead them over to the promised land. The Rock having been once smitten, there was no need to smite it again, but only to speak to it. So Christ, the Rock of our salvation having once died upon the Cross, now *once* hath appeared to put away sin by the sacrifice of Himself.

While the Lord says to those who love Him:—

Whatsoever ye shall *ask* in my Name, that will I do, that the Father may be glorified in the Son: If ye shall ask any thing in my Name, I will do it; (*John* xiv. 13, 14.) He saith also:—

What is this then that is written, The Stone which the builders rejected, the same is become the head of the corner? Whosoever shall fall upon that Stone shall be broken; but on whomsoever it shall fall, it will grind him to powder. *Luke* xx. 17, 18.

St. Paul calls the Church built upon this Rock:

The Church of the living God, the pillar and ground of the truth. 1 *Tim.* iii. 15.

The twentieth of the Articles of Religion, in the

Book of Common Prayer, says:—

Although the Church be a witness and a keeper of Holy Writ, yet, as it ought not to decree any thing against the same, so besides the same ought it not to enforce any thing to be believed for necessity of salvation.

We are taught to pray for this Church thus:—

LORD, we beseech thee to keep thy household the Church in continual godliness; that, through thy protection, it may be free from all adversities, and devoutly given to serve thee in good works, to the glory of thy name, through Jesus Christ our Lord. *Amen.*

CHAPTER XVI.

THE RESURRECTION OF THE BODY.

—:o:—

In accordance with the warnings which God had given to His chosen people, the *body* of the Church of Israel *died*, and its members were dispersed through all the world. There were left to them no holy city, no temple, no altar upon which the appointed sacrifices should be offered.

But the prophets say that the members of this Body shall be collected together again, and that it shall be as it were resuscitated, raised from the dead into new life. Ezekiel shows this by his parable of the dry bones:—

Then He said unto me, Son of man, these bones are the whole house of Israel: behold, they say, Our bones are dried, and our hope is lost: we are cut off for our parts. Therefore prophesy and say unto them, Thus saith the Lord God; Behold, O my people, I will open your graves, and cause you to come up out of your graves, and bring you into the land of Israel. And ye shall know that I am the Lord, when I have opened your graves, O my people, and brought you up out of your graves, and shall put my spirit in you, and ye shall live. *Ezek.* xxxvii. 11–14.

Isaiah says:—

It shall come to pass in that day, that the Lord shall set His hand again the second time to recover the remnant of His people, which shall be left.... And He shall set up an ensign for the nations, and shall assemble the outcasts of Israel, and gather together the dispersed of Judah from the four corners of the earth. *Isaiah* xi. 11, 12.

So Jeremiah:—

Therefore, behold, the days come, saith the Lord, that they shall no more say, The Lord liveth which brought up the children of Israel out of the land of Egypt; But, the Lord liveth, which brought up and which led the seed of the house of Israel out of the North country, and from all countries whither I had driven them; and they shall dwell in their own land. *Jer.* xxiii. 7, 8.

Again, Zechariah says:—

I will strengthen the house of Judah, and I will save the house of Joseph, and I will bring them again to place them; for I have mercy upon them: and they shall be as though I had not cast them off: for I am the Lord their God. *Zech.* x. 6.

St. Paul says:—

Israel hath not obtained that which he seeketh for; but the election hath obtained it, and the rest were blinded.... I say then, Have they stumbled that they should fall? God forbid: but rather through their fall salvation is come unto the Gentiles, for to provoke them to jealousy.... For if the casting away of them be the reconciling of the world, what shall the receiving of them be, but *life from the dead?* .... Thou wilt say then, The branches were broken off, that I might be graffed in. Well; because of unbelief they were broken off, and thou standest by faith.... And they also, if they abide not still in unbelief, shall be graffed in: for God is able to graff them in again. For if thou wert cut out of the olive tree which is wild by nature, and wert graffed contrary to nature into a good olive tree; how much more shall these, which be the natural branches, be graffed into their own olive tree? .... And so all Israel shall be saved. *Rom.* xi. 2–27.

The history of the Israelites is full of types; and it would seem not to be by accident that this one has been adopted by the Church in appointing to be read in her morning lesson for the Sunday before Ascension Day, when she celebrates the real resurrection of our Lord from the dead, that passage from Zechariah:—

Behold, I will save my people from the east country, and from the west country; and I will bring them, and they shall dwell in the midst of Jerusalem. *Zech.* viii. 7, 8.

And again she repeats the promise in the evening lesson:—

I will bring them again...... for I have redeemed them .... and they shall live with their children and turn again. *Zech.* x. 6–9.

What shall this receiving of them from their dispersed condition be but *life from the dead*, obtained, as St. Paul says, through the Deliverer coming out of Sion, our Saviour as well as theirs?

As if to show what the redemption and bringing again of the body of Israel should typify, the Church appoints her second evening Lesson to tell of our resurrection at the last day:—

As Jesus died and rose again, even so them also which sleep in Jesus will God bring with Him. 1 *Thess.* iv. 13.—Of the people of Israel St. Paul says:—

Even unto this day, when Moses is read, the vail is upon their heart. Nevertheless when it shall turn to the Lord, the vail shall be taken away. 2 *Cor.* iii. 13-16.—And of the Lord Jesus he says:—

He is the Head of the Body, the Church; who is the beginning, the firstborn from the dead. *Col.* i. 18.

Our Lord predicted His own death, and that He should also rise again:—

From that time forth began Jesus to show unto His disciples, how that He must go unto Jerusalem, and suffer many things of the elders and Chief Priests and Scribes, and be killed, and *be raised again* the third day. *Matt.* xvi. 21.

Hosea has a remarkable passage which is doubtless a prophecy that the Lord should rise on the third day:—

Come and let us return unto the Lord: for He hath torn and He will heal us; He hath smitten, and He will bind us up. After two days will He revive us: *in the third day He will raise us up,* and we shall live in His sight. *Hosea* vi. 1-3.

Isaiah has a similar passage:—

Thy dead men shall live, *together with my dead body shall they arise.* Awake and sing, ye that dwell in dust: for thy dew is as the dew of herbs, and the earth shall cast out the dead. *Isaiah* xxvi. 19.

The last time the Lord "shewed Himself alive after His passion," to His Apostles, (*Acts* i. 21.)

He said unto them, These are the words which I spake unto you, while I was yet with you, that all things must be fulfilled which were written in the law of Moses, and in the Prophets, and in the Psalms, concerning me. Then opened He their understanding, that they might understand the Scriptures, And said unto them, Thus it is written, and thus it behoved Christ to suffer, and to rise from the dead the third day: And that repentance of sins should be preached in His name among all nations.... And He led them out as far as to Bethany, and He lifted up His hands and blessed them. And it came to pass, while He blessed them, He was parted from them, and carried up into heaven. *Luke* xxiv. 44–51.

There are other instances of men ascending up to heaven.

Enoch walked with God: and he was not; for God took him. *Genesis* v. 24.—By faith Enoch was translated that he should not see death; and was not found because God had translated him: for before his translation he had this testimony, that he pleased God. *Hebrews* xi. 5.—Again :-

It came to pass, when the Lord would take up Elijah into heaven by a whirlwind, that Elijah went with Elisha from Gilgal...... And it came to pass, as they still went on, and talked, that, behold, there appeared a chariot of fire, and horses of fire, and parted them both asunder; and Elijah went up by a whirlwind into heaven. *2 Kings* ii. 1, 11.

That the spirit may be reunited to the body so as to make it alive again, is shown by our Lord's raising from the dead the daughter of Jairus. (*Mark* v. 35-42.) And the son of the widow of Nain. (*Luke* vii. 12-15.) And Lazarus, after he had been lying in the grave four days. (*John* xi. 1-44.)

And the graves were opened; and many bodies of the saints which slept arose, and came out of the graves after His resurrection, and went into the holy city, and appeared unto many. *Matt.* xxvii. 52, 53.

St. Paul very plainly preaches the doctrine of the resurrection in his first Epistle to the Corinthians, fifteenth chapter, (used in the Burial Service of the Church,) in which he adduces the operations of Nature as a proof that our natural bodies shall die, and see corruption, and be raised again.

God giveth it a body as it hath pleased Him, and to every seed his own body.... So is also the resurrection of the dead. It is sown in corruption; it is raised in incorruption: It is sown in dishonour; it is raised in glory: It is sown in weakness; it is raised in power. It is sown a natural body; it is raised a spiritual body. 1 *Cor.* xv. 38, 42-44.—Now :-

If we believe that Jesus died and rose again, even so them also which sleep in Jesus [they are of His Body, the Church,] will God bring with Him. For this we say unto you by the word of the Lord, that we which are alive and remain unto the coming of the Lord shall not prevent [*go before*] them which are asleep. For the Lord Himself shall descend from heaven with a shout, with the voice of the Archangel, and with the trump of God: and the dead in Christ shall rise first: Then we which are alive and remain shall be caught up together with them in the clouds to meet the Lord in the air: and so shall we ever be with the Lord. 1 *Thess.* iv. 14-17.

Thus there appears to be an allegorical connection between the promise that the body of the Jewish Church shall be collected and resuscitated a spiritual body, when it shall turn to the Lord Jesus in faith; and that the natural bodies of all those who die in Christ shall be raised up spiritual bodies, when He shall appear again.

The Church in her Creed says, "I look for the Resurrection of the dead, And the life of the world to come." And that we may apply the lessons taught by the Resurrection, she gives us this form of supplication in the Collect for Ascension Day:

GRANT, we beseech thee, Almighty God, that like as we do believe thy only begotten Son our Lord Jesus Christ to have ascended into the heavens; so we may also in heart and mind thither ascend, and with Him continually dwell, who liveth and reigneth with thee and the Holy Ghost, one God, world without end. *Amen.*

CHAPTER XVII.

UNITY.

———:o:———

While so much is said about Unity among the worshipers of God, and so much thought is given to discover the best way to bring it about, it is worth while to study what the Bible says upon the subject.

The idea of true unity centers in our Saviour Christ, who is the Head of the Body, the Church.

To Abraham and his Seed were the promises made. He saith not, And to seeds, as of many; but as of *one*. And to thy Seed, which is Christ. *Gal.* iii. 16.

Because of the fidelity of their father Abraham the Lord chose Israel to be one nation, separate from all other people of the world, to serve Him.

Moses went up unto God, and the Lord called unto him out of the mountain, saying, Thus shalt thou say to the house of Jacob, and tell the children of Israel... If ye will obey my voice indeed, and keep my covenant, then ye shall be *a peculiar treasure unto me above all people*: for all the earth is mine: and ye shall be unto me *a kingdom of priests, and an holy nation*. *Exodus* xix. 3-6.

The token of the covenant in which the children of Israel became members of this holy nation was circumcision. Provision was also made for strangers, or Gentiles, to become members of this holy nation through means of the same covenant token.

When a stranger shall sojourn with thee, and will keep the Passover to the Lord, let all his males be circumcised, and then let him come near and keep it; and he shall be as one that is born in the land: for no uncircumcised person shall eat thereof. *One law* shall be to him that is homeborn, and unto the stranger that sojourneth among you. *Exodus* xiii. 48, 49.

Thus saith the Lord.... Neither let the son of the stranger, that hath joined himself to the Lord, speak, saying, The Lord hath utterly separated me from His people.... for thus saith the Lord.... Also the sons of the stranger, that join themselves to the Lord, to serve Him, and to love the Name of the Lord, to be His servants, every one that keepeth the sabbath from polluting it, and taketh hold of my covenant; even them will I bring to my holy mountain, and make them joyful in my house of prayer: their burnt offerings and their sacrifices shall be accepted upon mine altar; for mine house shall be called an house of prayer *for all people.* The Lord God which gathereth the outcasts of Israel saith, Yet will I *gather others to Him, beside those that are gathered unto Him. Is.* lv. 1–8.—This promise to the Jewish Church was also made to the Christian Church:-

Then said Jesus unto them .... I am the good Shepherd, and know my sheep, and am known of mine. As the Father knoweth me, even so know I the Father. And *other sheep I have* which are not of this fold: *them also I must bring*, and they shall hear my voice; and there shall be *one fold*, and *one Shepherd.   John* x. 14–16.—But Moses says:-

Then there shall be *a place* which the Lord your God shall choose to cause His Name to dwell there; thither shall ye bring all that I command you, your burnt offerings, and your sacrifices, your tithes, and the heave offering of your hand, and all your choice vows which ye vow unto the Lord.... Take heed to thyself that thou offer not thy burnt offerings *in every place that thou seest*: But in the place which the Lord *shall choose* in one of thy tribes, there thou shalt offer thy burnt offerings, and there thou shalt do all that I command thee. *Deut.* xii. 11, 13.

And this was the place that the Lord chose:-

And thou shalt say unto them, Whatsoever man there be of the house of Israel, or of the strangers which sojourn among you, that offereth a burnt offering, or sacrifice, and bringeth it not unto *the door of the tabernacle of the congregation*, to offer it unto the

Lord; even that man shall be *cut off from among his people.* Levit. xvii. 8, 9.

When he had finished the temple at Jerusalem Solomon stood before the altar of the Lord in the presence of all the congregation of Israel, and spread forth his hands toward heaven: And he said, Lord God of Israel, there is no God like thee, in heaven above, or on earth beneath, who keepest covenant and mercy with thy servants that walk before thee with all their heart.... But will God indeed dwell on earth? behold, the heaven and heaven of heavens cannot contain thee; how much less this house that I have builded? Yet have thou respect unto the prayer of thy servant.... That thine eyes may be open toward *this house* night and day, even toward the place of which thou hast said, My Name shall be there: that thou mayest hearken unto the prayer which thy servant shall make toward this place. 1 *Kings* viii. 22–29.

Moreover concerning a stranger, that is not of thy people Israel, but cometh out of a far country for thy name's sake; (For they shall hear of thy great Name, and of thy strong hand, and of thy stretched out arm;) when he shall come and pray *toward this house;* Hear thou in heaven thy dwelling place, and do according to all that the stranger calleth to thee for: that all people of the earth may know thy name, to fear thee, as do thy people Israel; and that they may know that this house which I have builded, is called by thy name. 1 *Kings* viii. 41–43.

In whatever place the Hebrews happened to be, they were wont to turn towards the Temple at Jerusalem when they prayed. They also went up to Jerusalem to sacrifice at the Temple, and to keep the three principal feasts of the Passover, Pentecost, and Tabernacles.

Of Jesus it is said:—

His parents went to Jerusalem every year at the Feast of the Passover. And when He was twelve years old, they went up to Jerusalem after the custom of the feast. *Luke* ii. 42.

All this seems to indicate that there should be but one authoritative church, typified by the priesthood and temple at Jerusalem, in which God should be worshiped.

We first read of schism among the Hebrews in the reign of Rehoboam, the son of Solomon, when ten tribes of Israel revolted from him, leaving only the tribe of Judah and the small tribe of Benjamin subject to him. "So Israel rebelled against the house of David unto this day." And they made Jeroboam king over Israel. (1 *Ki.* xii. 1–20.)

The consequences of this schism immediately began to be seen:—

And Jeroboam said in his heart, Now shall the kingdom return to the house of David: If this people go up to do sacrifice in the house of the Lord at Jerusalem, then shall the heart of this people turn again unto their lord, even unto Rehoboam king of Judah, and they shall kill me.... Whereupon the king took counsel, and made two calves of gold, and said unto them, It is too much for you to go up to Jerusalem: behold thy gods, O Israel, which brought thee up out of the land of Egypt. And he set the one in Bethel, and the other put he in Dan. And *this thing became a sin*: for the people went to worship before the one, even unto Dan. And he made an house of high places, and *made priests of the lowest of the people*, which were not *of the sons of Levi.* 1 *Kings* xii. 26–31.

The unlawful sacrifices, and feasts, and incense before this altar were rebuked by a man of God who came out of Judah, and prophesied that a man named Josiah should come and burn those priests upon the altar; and the altar was rent. 1 *Kings* xiii. 1–5.

The schismatic tribes were always more prone to be idolatrous, and more easily led away from the true God, than Judah. After the separation of the twelve tribes dispersion became the doom of them all, for they wandered from the prescribed worship of God, and thus broke His covenant. They were also divided up into sects, such as the Pharisees, who were filled with pride and hypocrisy, and yet kept up the outward observance of the law with great ostentation. There were also the Sadduces who believed in no future rewards, or punishments; and others. There was yet after all, a remnant of true Israelites; and many of these became disciples of our Lord, while as a rule the Sects bitterly opposed Him.

Let us see if there are any warnings given to the Church of the new dispensation, to avoid the fate of the twelve tribes by watching lest:—

The time will come when they will not endure sound doctrine; but after their own lusts shall they *heap to themselves teachers,* having itching ears; And they shall turn away their ears from the truth, and shall be turned unto fables. 2 *Tim.* iv. 3, 4.

As Circumcision was the token of the covenant by which Jew and Stranger became members of the Church of Israel, so is Baptism with the Christian Church. Our Lord saith :—

Except a man be born of water and of the Spirit, he

cannot enter into the kingdom of God. *John* iii. 5.

The Christian Church is characterised in the same manner as the Church of Israel:-

Unto you therefore which believe, He [Christ] is precious...... But ye are *a chosen generation, a royal priesthood, an holy nation, a peculiar people*; that ye should shew forth the praises of Him who hath called you out of darkness into His marvellous light: Which in time past were not a people, but are now the people of God. 1 *Peter* ii. 7, 9, 10.

Now St. Paul says:-

As the body *is one*, and hath many members, and all the members of that one body, being many, *are one body*: So also is Christ. For by one Spirit *are we all baptized into one body*, whether we be Jews or Gentiles, whether we be bond or free. 1 *Cor*. 12, 13.

And He gave some, apostles; and some, prophets; and some, evangelists; and some, pastors and teachers; For the perfecting of the saints, for the work of the ministry, for the edifying of the body of Christ: Till we all come in [or, into. *Marg*.] the *unity of the faith*, and of the knowledge of the Son of God, unto a perfect man, unto the measure of the stature of the fulness of Christ: That we henceforth be no more children tossed to and fro, and carried about with *every wind of doctrine*, by the sleight of men, and cunning craftiness, whereby they lie in wait to deceive; But speaking the truth in love, may grow up into Him in all things, which is the head, even Christ. *Eph*. iv. 11-15.—The idea of UNITY runs through all these texts; and the Apostles continually press it upon all the believers in Christ. Thus St. Paul in the following passages:-

The cup of blessing which we bless, is it not the

Communion of the blood of Christ? The bread which we break, is it not the Communion of the body of Christ? For we being many, are *one bread, and one body*: for we are all partakers of that *one bread*. 1 Cor. x. 16, 17.

For as we have many members *in one body*, and all members have not the same office: so we being many, are *one body* in Christ, and every one members one of another. Rom. xii. 4, 5.

I therefore, the prisoner of the Lord, beseech you that ye walk worthy of the vocation wherewith ye are called, with all lowliness and meekness, with longsuffering, forbearing one another in love; endeavouring *to keep the unity of the Spirit* in the bond of peace. There is *one* body, and *one* Spirit, even as ye are called in *one* hope of your calling; *one* Lord, *one* faith, *one* baptism, *one* God and Father of *all*. Eph. iv. 1-6.

Be of the *same mind* one toward another. Rom. xii. 16.

If there be therefore any consolation in Christ, if any comfort of love, if any fellowship of the Spirit.... fulfil ye my joy, that ye be *likeminded*, having the same love, being of *one accord*, of *one mind*. Phil. ii. 1, 2.—Finally, brethren, farewell. Be perfect, be of good comfort, be *of one mind*, live in peace; and the God of love and peace shall be with you. 2 Cor. xiii. 11.—Only let your conversation be as becometh the Gospel of Christ: that whether I come and see you, or else be absent, I may hear of your affairs, that ye stand fast in *one spirit*, with *one mind* striving together for the faith of the Gospel. Phil. i. 27.

And St. Peter says:—

Finally, be ye all of *one mind*, having compassion one of another, love as brethren. 1 Peter iii. 8.

But unity is not only to have one mind, one spirit; for St. Paul says:—

Now the God of patience and consolation grant you to be likeminded one toward another according to Christ Jesus: that ye may with one mind and one *mouth* [by the use of *forms?* How else?] glorify God, even the Father of our Lord Jesus Christ. *Rom.* xv. 5, 6.—So it is said of "all that believed":—

They, continuing daily with *one accord* in the temple, and breaking bread from house to house, did eat their meat with gladness and singleness of heart, praising God, and having favour with the people; and the Lord added *to the Church* daily such as should be saved. *Acts* ii. 46.

And the multitude of them that believed were of one heart and of one soul. *Acts* iv. 32.

Our blessed Lord prayed:—

Holy Father, keep through thine own Name those whom thou hast given me, that they may be *one, as we are*.... Neither pray I for these alone, but for them also which shall believe on me through their word; That they *all may be one*; as thou, Father, art in me, and I in thee, that they also may be *one with us*: that the world may believe that thou hast sent me. *John* xvii. 11, 20, 21.

In any religious body where all hold the same opinions, there is a warm sympathy between its members. What the Lord and His holy Apostles would have is, that the same affectionate concord should exist between *all* of His followers. Hence the absolute necessity for UNITY in order that the Lord's will may be really complied with.

Before sects, or denominations, had arisen in the Christian Church, St. Paul uttered this earnest and prophetic warning:—

Now I beseech you, brethren, by the Name of our Lord Jesus Christ, that ye all speak the same thing, and that there be no divisions [or, schisms. *Marg.*] among you; but that ye be perfectly joined together in the same mind and in the same judgment. For it hath been declared unto me of you, my brethren..... that there are contentions among you. Now this I say, that every one of you saith, I am of Paul; and I of Apollos; and I of Cephas; and I of Christ. Is Christ divided? 1 *Cor.* i. 10–13.

God hath tempered the body together.... that there should be no *schism* in the body; but that the members should have the same care one for another.... Now ye are the body of Christ, and members in particular. 1 *Corinthians* xii. 24, 25, 27.

Our Lord said:—

Every kingdom divided against itself is brought to desolation; and a house divided against a house falleth. *Luke* xi. 17.

So eventually did the house of Israel; though not till after many years, and many warnings.

Solomon, the wise man, says:—

These six things doth the Lord hate...... he that soweth discord among brethren. *Prov.* vi. 16, 19.

And St. Paul says:—

Now I beseech you, brethren, mark them which cause *divisions* and offences contrary to the doctrine which ye have learned; and avoid them. For they that are such serve not our Lord Jesus Christ, but their own belly: and by good words and fair speeches deceive the hearts of the simple. *Rom.* xvi. 17, 18.

Ye are yet carnal: for whereas there is among you envying, and strife, and *divisions* [or, factions. *Marg.*]

are ye not carnal, and walk as men? For while one saith, I am of Paul; and another, I am of Apollos; are ye not carnal? 1 *Cor.* iii. 3, 4.

St. Mark relates that when Jesus was passing over the sea in a ship, "there were also with Him other *little ships.*" *Mark* iv. 36.

David says, "The mountains also shall bring peace, and the *little hills* righteousness unto the people." *Psalm* lxxii. 3.

St. Paul declares, "For there must be also heresies [or, sects. *Marg.*] among you, that they which are approved may be made manifest among you." 1 *Cor.* xi. 19.

If the ship and the mountain stand for the Church; and the little ships and the little hills for the Sects, then here, possibly, is a reason for the present want of unity. Though all may accompany the Lord, and may bring righteousness unto the people, yet there ought not to be any schism in the body of Christ; for "He is the head of the Body, the Church," and how can He be divided? Nevertheless, their existence causes a closer study and better understanding of the Bible; and a trial of each system by it as the only safe standard, Till "all come in the unity of the faith, and of the knowledge of the Son of God."

Lest the unity of the Lord's Body should be broken, St. Paul gives to Titus this warning command:—

This is a faithful saying; and these things I will that thou affirm constantly; that they which have believed in God might be careful to maintain good works. These things are good and profitable unto men. But *avoid foolish questions*, and genealogies, *and conten-*

tions, and strivings about the law; for they are unprofitable and vain. *Titus* iii. 8, 9.

In view of these frequent exhortations to unity it would seem that there must now be a Church of divine sanction, if not of divine authority, in which all believers in the Bible can rally in unity. That such is the case seems to be taught by the Lord's miracle of the net enclosing a multitude of fishes: For all there were so many yet was not the net broken. *John* xxi. 6-11.

So also by St. Peter's vision, in which he:—
Saw heaven opened, and a certain vessel descending unto him, as it had been a great sheet, knit at the four corners, and let down to the earth; Wherein were all manner of fourfooted beasts of the earth, and wild beasts and creeping things, and fowls of the air. *Acts* x. 9-16.

Is not this the Church gathered from the four corners of the earth, into which all who believe may enter, and none may call them common or unclean? The Church prays: "From all false doctrine, heresy and schism, Good Lord, deliver us; And this is her "Prayer for all Conditions of Men:"—

O GOD, the Creator and Preserver of all mankind, we humbly beseech thee for all sorts and conditions of men, that thou wouldest be pleased to make thy ways known unto them, thy saving health unto all nations. More especially we pray for thy holy Church universal; that it may be so guided and governed by thy good Spirit, that all who profess and call themselves Christians, may be led into the way of truth, and hold the faith *in unity of Spirit,* in the bond of peace, and in righteousness of life. Finally, we commend to thy Fatherly goodness, all those who are any ways afflicted or distressed in mind, body, or estate; that it may please thee to comfort and relieve them, according to their several necessities: giving them patience under their sufferings, and a happy issue out of all their afflictions: and this we beg for Jesus Christ's sake. *Amen.*

CHAPTER XVIII.

THE BOOK OF COMMON PRAYER.

—:o:—

In no way are the harmonies of the Bible and the Church more beautifully and more plainly illustrated, than in the use of the Book of Common Prayer. As a guide in the worship of Almighty God, it systematically teaches the true relation of the Church to her Saviour and Head; to God the Father Son and Holy Ghost.

Nor is it necessary to restrict the use of it to *public* worship. There is hardly a proper emotion or aspiration of the heart which does not find expression in some prayer or collect; and thus are offered to one who is slow of speech the very words he needs in his secret communion with his Lord. Such use of the forms of prayer in private devotions, tends to a better apprehension of their import, which enhances their benefit when we join in the public services of the Church.

The ritual of the Church of Israel, embracing the sacrifices, purifications, fasts, &c. was given by God in a special revelation to Israel. He informed them that these observances were *typical* and imperfect. (*Heb.* ix. x.) They were to continue in a form addressed to the outward senses, as *shadows* of the heavenly things, until the Messiah should come to do away with their imperfect priesthood, and to substitute spiritual sacrifices for the sensual types. Is not the discontinuance of the sacrifices for so long, without a sign of their being renewed, a proof that the Messiah has already come?

Would it not be natural to look for a continuation of the Church of Israel, in a form which in its ritual should present a spiritual worship fulfilling the types of the Old Testament, and obeying the injunction, to keep them as a statute for ever? The extent to which the use of the Book of Common Prayer complies with that condition is probably realized by but few of those who use it most and love it best. Our Lord said, "Think not that I am come to destroy the law, or the prophets: I am not come to destroy, but to fulfil." *Matt.* v. 17. So the Church seeks to fulfil the law in all things.

It fulfils the law concerning the Priesthood, having three orders of its Ministry, corresponding to the three Jewish orders.

It has the Sacrament of Baptism, by which persons become members of it, (*John* iii. 5.) corresponding to the Jewish rite of Circumcision.

Also the Lord's Supper, corresponding to the Jewish sacrifice of the lamb.

Then it has the three principal annual Feasts, corresponding to those which the Jews were commanded to keep: Easter for the Passover; Whitsuntide for Pentecost; Christmas for the Tabernacles.

The prayers, collects, &c. are made up of texts of Scripture. (*See Scripture proofs of the Liturgy, by Rev. Dr. Benj. Hale.*) Thus they teach how to pray for what the Bible tells us we need, in the very words of the Bible itself. When His disciples said, "Lord, teach us how to pray," Jesus replied, "When ye pray, say, Our Father which art in heaven," &c. Accordingly, in every separate office in the Book of Common Prayer; as well as in the form for Morning and Evening Prayer, the Lord's Prayer is appointed to be said.

Again, our Lord said to His disciples, "Whatsoever ye shall ask the Father in my Name, He will give it you." Accordingly, each prayer ends with a sentence such as this: "Through Jesus Christ, our Lord." So the prayers teach us our duty, and make us ask for grace to do it.

By the division of the year into seasons, and setting apart certain holidays, according to the tables in the beginning of the Prayer Book, all the prominent events, and doctrines of the Bible are week after week, presented in four appropriate chapters of the Bible, and in the Epistle and Gospel for the day, so selected that by comparison they illustrate some particular subject. Thus the Church as it were *acts out* every year, the story of the Gospel, beginning with the birth of the Saviour, at the season of Advent and Christmas, and occupying about half of the year, after Trinity, in a miscellaneous review.

One great benefit of this system is the practical way in which the discipline of the Church forms the spirit of man in accord with the Holy Spirit, by inspiration of whom all holy Scripture is written. As an illustration; The services in Passion week bring the Lord's passion as vividly to mind as it is possible for words to do. By strict attention to them, the subject assumes such a form of reality that we seem to have had all the events enacted before our eyes. It is in this way that the Church educates her children in faith. By *spiritually* enacting the great scenes of the Bible at stated seasons, and in such a systematic manner, the truth and reality of them all is made familiar to the mind from childhood, and faith in them is steadily developed and confirmed.

The same is quite true in regard to the denunciations against sin, and the promised rewards for a holy life, which have their due prominence, especially at the seasons set apart for self examination and discipline.

So in the use of the Psalter. The Psalms were sung by the Jews at their daily worship in the Temple. They had a regular choir of singers, accompanied by players on instruments. (1 *Chron.* vi. 31, 32.–xxv. 1-7.) Beside the daily service of song, they had special psalms for particular occasions. A few instances of similar use of the same psalms by the Church, will suffice.

In the Bible version, a title is given to Psalm xcii: "A Psalm or Song for the Sabbath Day." It begins thus: "It is a good thing to give thanks unto the Lord." This Psalm is supposed to have been composed by David, after he had rest from all his enemies, (2 *Sam.* vii. 1.) or about the time that the Ark was conveyed to Mount Zion, to be used in the worship of the Sanctuary on the Sabbath Day. It was always sung by the Jewish choirs on that day. A portion of this psalm is a chaunt appointed for the daily Evening Prayer, and is an echo to the exhortation at the beginning of the service: "To render thanks for the great benefits that we have received at His hands, to set forth His most worthy praise."

Every person may find in the Psalter for the day some thing peculiarly suited to his own secret feelings, and may appropriate to himself the words which David uttered, and the Church of Israel sang. One who is suffering under sorrow, temptation, or sin, and is trying to bear or to resist it by his own strength, may find a solution of his difficulties at Evening Prayer the sixth day of the month, in Psalm xxxii; which was composed by David in reference to his interview with the prophet Nathan. 2 *Sam.* xii.

An instance of the Church acting out a grand historical type of the Bible, is found in the use of Psalm xxiv. as one of the proper psalms for Ascension Day, at Evening Prayer. The bringing of the Ark of the covenant—the visible token of God's presence with His people—to Mount Zion, (1 *Chron.* xv.) gave occasion for this Psalm. The removal of the Ark was attended by a magnificent procession of the people, as many as could be assembled for the purpose. "There was little Benjamin with their ruler, the princes of Judah and their council, the princes of Zebulun, and the princes of Napthali." (*Psalm* lxviii. 27.) "The Levites led the procession, accompanied by a great variety of vocal and instrumental music."

The children of the Levites bear the Ark of God upon their shoulders, with the staves thereon, as Moses commanded according to the word of the Lord. 1 *Chron.* xv. 15.

They have seen Thy goings, O God; the goings of my God, my King, in the Sanctuary. The singers go before, the players on instruments after; among them were the damsels playing with timbrels. *Ps.* lxviii.

And as they went they chaunted psalms. On arriving at the summit of the mountain upon which stood the Tabernacle, they sang:—

The earth is the Lord's, and all that therein is; the compass of the world, and they that dwell therein.

Thus they proclaimed the almighty power of Him whose servants they were.

Who shall ascend into the hill of the Lord? or who shall rise up in His holy place?

Who is worthy thus to do Him service?

Even he that hath clean hands and a pure heart.... he shall receive the blessing from the Lord.

And now they drew near the Tabernacle, and beheld its spacious gates; and the Levites sang aloud:

Lift up your heads, O ye gates; and be ye lift up, ye everlasting doors; and the King of Glory shall come in!

Then the gate keepers challenged:—

Who is this King of Glory?

And the Levites replied:—

It is the Lord strong and mighty, even the Lord mighty in battle. Even the Lord of hosts. He is the King of Glory.

And so the grand procession passed in, and the Ark of God was "set in the midst of the tent that David had pitched for it." 1 *Chron.* xvi. 1.

And now the Church teaches us to turn to that

spot near Bethany, whither our blessed Saviour led His disciples, and lifted up His hands and blessed them.

And it came to pass, while He blessed them, He was parted from them, and carried up into heaven. *Luke* xxiv. 50, 51.

Can we not imagine Him borne upwards, flying "upon the wings of the wind," (*Ps.* xviii. 10.) triumphantly ascending amidst myriads of ministering angels, to that Holy City whose foundations are garnished with precious stones, whose twelve gates are twelve pearls, whose streets are pure gold; and the Lord God Almighty and the Lamb are the Temple of it! (*Rev.* xxi.)

As the glorious company gains the precious gates, there arises this shout of triumph–triumph for us, because our Saviour hath "overcome death and opened unto us the gate of everlasting life" (*Collect for Easter.*):–

Lift up your heads, O ye gates; and be ye lift up, ye everlasting doors; and the King of Glory shall come in!

And to the responsive shout, "Who is this King of Glory?" swells the grand chorus which echoes from the remotest corners of the earth, and is taken up by "the holy Church throughout all the world:"–

It is the Lord strong and mighty; the Lord mighty in battle; the Lord of hosts; He is the King of Glory!

Let us now examine the offices, or "ministrations," appointed for the rites and ceremonies of the Church.

In the "Order for the administration of the Lord's Supper, or Holy Communion," it is difficult to select any one part more than another to show the harmony between the Bible and the Church. Perhaps it is most conspicuous in the "Prayer of Consecration," and in the one immediately preceding, to be said by the Minister "in the name of all those who shall receive the Communion."

The Prayer in the "Ministration of Baptism," beautifully sets forth the type of the Ark built by Noah, "wherein few, that is, eight souls were saved *by water*. The like figure whereunto even baptism doth now save us." 1 *Peter* iii. 20, 21.

The Ark typifies the Church, into which having entered by *water*, we may be saved through obedience to its teaching and ordinances (that is by keeping within its shelter,) from being destroyed by the raging storms of temptation and trial.

The Prayer likewise illustrates the figure which St. Paul uses :–

Moreover brethren, I would not that ye should be ignorant, how that all our fathers were under the cloud and all passed through the sea; And were all *baptized* unto Moses in the cloud and in the sea. 1 *Cor*. x.

"The Order of Confirmation" is in harmony with the consecration of a Priest, with laying on of hands by the Bishop, to minister in the Church; for a person is in like manner consecrated as a priest over his own body, which is the temple of the Lord. (*See pp*. 105–108.) The Jews had a rite similar to Confirmation, to which it is supposed that Jesus submitted when He was twelve years old. *Luke* ii. 43.

In the exhortation in the "Form of Solemnization of Matrimony," matrimony is said to be :–
Commended of St. Paul to be honourable among

all men: and therefore is not by any to be entered into unadvisedly or lightly; but reverently, discreetly, advisedly, soberly, and in the fear of God.

St. Paul thus explains the solemn typical significance of marriage:—

Wives, submit yourselves unto your own husbands, as unto the Lord. For the husband is the head of the wife, even as Christ is the head of the Church: and He is the Saviour of the body. Therefore as the Church is subject unto Christ, so let wives be to their own husbands in every thing. Husbands, love your wives, even as Christ also loved the Church, and gave Himself for it: So ought men to love their wives as their own bodies. He that loveth his wife loveth himself. For no man ever yet hated his own flesh; but nourisheth and cherisheth it, even as the Lord the Church. For we are members of His Body, of His *flesh, and of His bones.* For this cause shall a man leave his father and mother, and shall be joined unto his wife, and they two shall be one flesh. This is a great mystery: but I speak concerning Christ and the Church. *Eph.* v. 22–32.

St. Paul here shows the type of the man Adam, and the woman Eve, taken out of his side:—

And Adam said, This is now *bone of my bones, and flesh of my flesh*: she shall be called Woman, because she was taken out of man. Therefore shall a man leave his father and his mother, and shall cleave unto his wife: and they shall be *one flesh*. *Gen.* ii. 23, 24.

This is the vow made at the time of marriage:—

Wilt thou have this Woman to thy wedded Wife, to live together after God's ordinance, in the holy estate of Matrimony? Wilt thou love her, comfort her, honour and keep her, in sickness and in health; and forsaking all others, keep thee only unto her, so long as ye both shall live?

In the "Order for the visitation of the sick," and in the Prayer "for persons under sentence of death," the form of blessing is used which:—

The Lord spake unto Moses, saying, Speak unto Aaron and unto his sons, saying, On this wise ye shall bless the children of Israel, saying unto them, The Lord bless thee, and keep thee: the Lord make His face shine upon thee, and be gracious unto thee: The Lord lift up His countenance upon thee, and give thee peace. *Num.* vi. 22–26.

The form of blessing pronounced when the Congregation is about to depart, is taken from what St. Paul says:—

And the peace of God which passeth all understanding, shall keep your hearts and minds through Jesus Christ. *Phil.* iv. 7.

These few examples may serve to aid in studying the *external means* appointed in the Church to interpret and apply the requirements of the Bible. By a faithful use of them we may realize the fulfilment of the Lord's promise, that the Comforter, which is the Holy Ghost, shall teach us all things. Many of the Collects contain petitions for it. The one to be said in the Communion Service, before the Ten Commandments, while it is a response to the exhortation at the opening of Morning and Evening Prayer—That we should not dissemble nor cloak our sins before the face of Almighty God our heavenly Father—is a prayer for this inestimable gift:—

ALMIGHTY God, unto whom all hearts are open, all desires known, and from whom no secrets are hid; cleanse the thoughts of our hearts by the inspiration of thy Holy Spirit; that we may perfectly love thee, and worthily magnify thy holy Name, through Christ our Lord. *Amen.*

If ye know these things, happy are ye if ye do them. *John* xiii. 17.

THE END.

---

www.ingramcontent.com/pod-product-compliance
Lightning Source LLC
Chambersburg PA
CBHW020253170426
43202CB00008B/357